HANDBOOK ON
ANTI-MONEY LAUNDERING
AND COMBATING THE
FINANCING OF TERRORISM

for Nonbank Financial Institutions

ASIAN DEVELOPMENT BANK

Creative Commons Attribution 3.0 IGO license (CC BY 3.0 IGO)

© 2017 Asian Development Bank

6 ADB Avenue, Mandaluyong City, 1550 Metro Manila, Philippines
Tel +63 2 632 4444; Fax +63 2 636 2444
www.adb.org

Some rights reserved. Published in 2017.
Printed in the Philippines.

ISBN 978-92-9257-761-2 (Print), 978-92-9257-762-9 (e-ISBN)
Publication Stock No. TIM168550
http://dx.doi.org/10.22617/TIM168550

Cataloging-In-Publication Data

Asian Development Bank.
　　Handbook on anti-money laundering and combating the financing of terrorism for nonbank financial institutions.
Mandaluyong City, Philippines: Asian Development Bank, 2017.

1. Anti-money laundering.　　2. Combating the financing of terrorism.　　I. Asian Development Bank.

The views expressed in this publication are those of the authors and do not necessarily reflect the views and policies of the Asian Development Bank (ADB) or its Board of Governors or the governments they represent.

ADB does not guarantee the accuracy of the data included in this publication and accepts no responsibility for any consequence of their use. The mention of specific companies or products of manufacturers does not imply that they are endorsed or recommended by ADB in preference to others of a similar nature that are not mentioned.

By making any designation of or reference to a particular territory or geographic area, or by using the term "country" in this document, ADB does not intend to make any judgments as to the legal or other status of any territory or area.

Note: Figures, tables, and boxes without explicit sources are those of ADB.
Corrigenda to ADB publications may be found at http://www.adb.org/publications/corrigenda

 Printed on recycled paper

Contents

Foreword iv

Abbreviations v

Overview 1

Part A: Policies and Standards 7
Roles and Responsibilities 9
Policy Statement 10
Customer Acceptance Policy 11
Independent Audit and Review 12
Risk-Based Approach to Managing Risk 13
Awareness Raising and Training of the Staff 23

Part B: Procedures 27
Customer Due Diligence Requirements 29
Requirements for Establishing a Relationship or Opening an Account 31
Reviewing Customer Due Diligence Information and Monitoring
    Customer Accounts 42
Recognizing Suspicious Activity 46
Record Keeping 49

Glossary 51

Appendixes
1   Responsibilities and Roles of Directors and Senior Management 53
2   Responsibilities and Roles of the Compliance Officer 55
3   Responsibilities and Roles of the Management 57
4   Responsibilities and Roles of the Staff 58
5   Example of a Risk Assessment Form 59
6   Example of an Account Opening Checklist—Individuals 62
7   Example of an Account Opening Checklist—Businesses 64
8   Examples of Suspicious Transactions 65
9   Web References 84

References 87

iii

Foreword

Nonbank financial institutions (NBFIs) serve as a viable option to banks by providing financial services to boost economic activity. They have expanded rapidly since the 2008/09 global financial crisis. Given the growing importance of NBFIs in facilitating access to finance and financial services, it becomes increasingly imperative for them to comply with anti-money laundering and combating the financing of terrorism (AML/CFT) requirements to avoid abuse by criminals or those involved in the financing of terrorism.

The Asian Development Bank (ADB), through its Office of Anticorruption and Integrity (OAI), has recognized the challenges facing NBFIs in meeting national and international AML/CFT requirements. Accordingly, ADB decided to develop a technical assistance project designed to develop AML/CFT approaches, methodologies, and controls for NBFIs. This handbook was developed under the auspices of the technical assistance commissioned by OAI. The purpose of the handbook is to assist NBFIs in developing and implementing internal policies, procedures, and controls, as well as to provide guidance on practical issues to manage the risks of being exposed to money laundering and the financing of terrorism.

This publication reflects the requirements of the international standard setter, the Financial Action Task Force, in the fight against money laundering and terrorist financing. Controls, policies, and procedures that should be implemented by individual NBFIs need to (i) reflect the requirements in their jurisdiction and (ii) be consistent with best practice and the NBFI's nature and scope of activities.

ADB hopes this handbook will be useful in your efforts to ensure that your institution is not used to launder the proceeds of crime or to finance terrorism.

Clare Wee
Head
Office of Anticorruption and Integrity
Asian Development Bank

Abbreviations

AML   anti-money laundering
CDD   customer due diligence
CFT   combating the financing of terrorism
FATF   Financial Action Task Force
NBFI   nonbank financial institution
PEP   politically exposed person

Overview

This handbook provides guidance to nonbank financial institutions (NBFIs) on how to manage risks related to money laundering and the financing of terrorism.

It comprises two parts. Part A outlines policies and standards that should be adopted by NBFIs and that reflect the international requirements of the Financial Action Task Force. Part B includes guidance on procedures that need to be implemented to ensure compliance with these requirements and those of the country's laws.

This handbook also serves as the basis for staff training.

How to use this handbook

This handbook is intended to assist NBFIs in developing and implementing policies and procedures to combat money laundering and the financing of terrorism. The handbook provides general guidance on key anti-money laundering and combating the financing of terrorism (AML/CFT) requirements. Information contained in the handbook should be adapted to reflect the nature of activities, products, and services offered by individual NBFIs as there is no "one size fits all" approach to the management of risk. Topics covered include information on the following:

- What is money laundering and terrorist financing?
- Why are NBFIs required to implement AML/CFT policies and procedures?
- The roles and responsibilities of senior management and staff of NBFIs
- The need to identify and understand risks
- The need to train staff
- Customer due diligence requirements
- Suspicious transaction identification and reporting
- Record-keeping obligations

The handbook includes examples of account opening forms and other information that may assist NBFIs in implementing effective AML/CFT risk management systems and controls.

Why are NBFIs covered by AML/CFT requirements?

NBFIs provide a range of financial services to their customers, which include

- the acceptance of deposits or other repayable funds from customers;
- lending;
- money or value transfer services;
- issuing and managing means of payment (e.g., credit and debit cards, checks, traveler's checks, money orders, and electronic money); and
- money and currency changing.

These financial services are subject to laws that deal with AML/CFT. These laws impose a range of requirements on NBFIs and these are outlined in this handbook.

What should NBFIs do to comply with AML/CFT requirements?

To comply with government legislation,[1] NBFIs must develop policies and procedures which will enable them to identify risks related to money laundering and terrorist financing and put in place controls to manage these risks, including the reporting of suspicious transactions to appropriate authorities. The policies and procedures which should be put in place include the following requirements:

- Assessing and understanding the risks arising from doing business
- Know your customer and customer due diligence (CDD)
- Monitoring transactions
- Reporting suspicious transactions
- Record keeping

If the government has approved legislation for tackling AML/CFT in its jurisdiction, the enforcement will be the responsibility of the supervisory authority and the financial intelligence unit.

---

[1] Subject to a country's own legislation.

What is money laundering and terrorism financing?

Money laundering

Money laundering means the ways in which criminals change "dirty" money and other assets into "clean" money or assets that have no obvious links to their criminal origin.

The three basic stages of money laundering are

i. **Placement.** During placement, "dirty" money derived from criminal activities is placed in the financial system.

ii. **Layering.** To conceal the illegal origin of the placed funds and thereby make them more useful to criminals, the funds must be moved, dispersed, and disguised. Layering is the process of disguising the source of the funds through layers of financial transactions.

iii. **Integration.** Once the funds are layered and can no longer be traced back to their criminal origins, they are integrated into the financial system and now appear "clean" and available for use by criminals. If layering has been successful, integration places the laundered money back into the economy and financial system in such a way that they appear as clean and legitimate.

Figure 1: A Typical Money-Laundering Scheme

PLACEMENT	LAYERING
Collection of "dirty" money	"Dirty" money integrates into the financial system	Transfer into bank account of company "X."

INTEGRATION		
Purchase of luxury assets; financial investments	Loan to company "Y" and payment of false invoice to company "X."	Wire transfer to offshore bank

Source: Adapted from the United Nations Office on Drugs and Crime.

Terrorism financing

Terrorist financing involves dealing with money or property that may be used for financing terrorist activities. The funds and property may be from either legitimate or criminal sources. They may be small amounts.

The methods used by terrorists to move money are substantially the same as those used by other criminals, such as the following:

Traditional financial institutions: Financial institutions are vulnerable to abuse by terrorists. Despite doing all that is required with respect to CDD, transactions related to the financing of terrorism may fail to set off any alarms or "red flags." For example, accounts can be opened, and small withdrawals and deposits which are less than any legal reporting requirements can be made.

Alternative remittance systems: Unregulated remittance systems such as *hawala* and *hundi*. These systems often have traditional roots or ethnic ties and operate in places where the formal finance sector is less established; funds can be transferred without any documentation.

Cash couriers: Cash is smuggled across borders, for example through land crossings and sea shipments where borders are uncontrolled.

False invoicing: False trade invoicing provides a means to transfer money between jurisdictions by overstating the value of the goods or services for which payment is due.

High-value commodities: Commodities like gold and diamonds can also be used to transfer value across borders as both are easy to convert into cash.

What are the penalties for not complying with AML/CFT requirements?

Usually, a country's legislation imposes a range of penalties if an NBFI fails to make a report on suspicious activity or activities relating to money laundering or the financing of terrorism; if they disclose any person that have made, or intend to make, such a report; or if it does not comply with the reporting requirements and other requirements related to record keeping and CDD implementation.

The penalties, which apply to both the staff and the NBFI, can include sanctions being imposed on the NBFI, financial penalties, criminal prosecution, or both, resulting in fines and/or imprisonment.

Part A
POLICIES AND STANDARDS

T o comply with anti-money laundering and combating the financing of terrorism (AML/CFT) requirements, staff within the nonbank financial institution (NBFI) need to be assigned roles and responsibilities to ensure that the NBFI's products and services are not used to launder money derived from criminal activities or to finance terrorism or terrorist activities. In addition to assigning roles and responsibilities to staff, NBFIs need to develop policies and standards which are effectively implemented.

These policies and standards deal with issues that may arise from customer acceptance policies, the need for a compliance function, and independent audit or review to ensure that policies and procedures are effectively implemented.

Even if the law does not impose specific requirements on directors, senior management, and staff or require the appointment of an AML/CFT compliance officer, it is best practice that NBFI staff implement policies and standards to ensure that the institution's products and services are not used to launder money or to finance terrorism. Such policies and standards, like other policies and procedures which govern the NBFI's day-to-day activities and dealings, are consistent with the requirements and expectations of both supervisory agencies and customers alike.

Roles and Responsibilities

Directors and senior management

Senior managers of NBFIs could be personally liable if they do not take the necessary steps to protect the business from money laundering or terrorist financing.

"Senior management" under the legislation could be defined to include a person in the NBFI, including any partner in a partnership, or a sole proprietor, with management responsibilities, including having primary responsibility for

- high-level decision making;
- implementing strategies and policies approved by the institution's board;

- developing processes that identify, manage, and monitor risks incurred by the institution; and
- monitoring the appropriateness, adequacy, and effectiveness of the risk management system.

The responsibilities and roles of directors and senior managers are outlined in Appendix 1.

Compliance officer

A compliance officer is appointed by the senior management as required by the law.

The compliance officer should have the appropriate background, skills, and experience required to ensure the effective performance of his or her duties.

The responsibilities and roles of the compliance officer are outlined in Appendix 2.

Management

Members of the management are responsible for ensuring that staff adhere consistently to the NBFI's policies and procedures to prevent money laundering and terrorist financing.

The responsibilities and roles of the management are outlined in Appendix 3.

Employees

Employees should carry out their duties in accordance with the NBFI's AML and counterterrorist financing procedures.

Further details of the responsibilities of employees are outlined in Appendix 4.

Policy Statement

This policy statement outlines policies and standards that are to be followed by employees when dealing with customers and/or when carrying out transactions. It requires the following

- The staff should only deal with those customers or conduct only those transactions that are consistent with the NBFI's customer acceptance policy.
- The staff identify customers, monitor their transactions, and take steps to mitigate the risk of the business being used for money laundering or terrorist financing.
- The senior management approves transactions and/or acceptance of customers in certain circumstances.
- The transactions must be monitored to ensure that they are consistent with staff knowledge of the customer and/or business activities and risk profile, including where necessary, the source of funds.
- Additional CDD checks and ongoing monitoring of customers and transactions are applied to high-risk customers.
- The compliance officer receives reports of suspicious activity and, after assessing these reports, forwards these reports to the financial intelligence unit.
- The staff are trained to recognize suspicious activities and to know what they should do if they suspect that a customer is attempting to launder funds or is involved in the financing of terrorism, including submitting reports of suspicious activity to the compliance officer.
- The records on customers and transactions are kept as required by the law.
- The implementation of the NBFI's policies and procedures are subject to review by an independent person, such as the internal auditor or an external auditor.

Customer Acceptance Policy

Senior management of the NBFI should determine that the NBFI will not accept as customers, or conduct transactions with, persons in the following circumstances:

- The customer has been identified by reliable sources as being a criminal or being associated with criminal groups.
- The customer has been identified by reliable sources as being a terrorist or being associated with a terrorist group or activities.

- The customer is from a jurisdiction identified by reliable sources as one that has high levels of criminal or terrorist activity(ies).
- The customer is involved in certain criminal or other such activities (e.g., prostitution) that are considered to be of high risk, given the nature of the source of funds.
- The customer is from a jurisdiction where there is a significant amount of corruption or other such activity(ies) (e.g., sale of illegal drugs and other such substances).
- The customer has been the subject of request from the financial intelligence unit (or law enforcement agencies).
- The customer is from a jurisdiction which has been identified as an area of high risk by the financial intelligence unit and/or the supervisory authority.
- The customer is from a jurisdiction which the NBFI has identified as not having implemented AML/CFT requirements that are consistent with those policies and procedures followed by the NBFI.
- The staff have reason to believe, based on the behavior of the customer or other factors (e.g., failure to provide an adequate reason for wishing to conduct the transaction or failure to disclose the source of funds), that the transaction may be related to money laundering or the financing of terrorism.

Independent Audit and Review

There should be an independent review of the NBFI's AML/CFT program, at least once every year. The review should cover the following areas and be performed in accordance with the established audit procedures, including review of samples of transactions and of account opening documentation.

The review of the compliance program should cover the following:

- customer identification and verification;
- suspicious transaction reporting (including other reporting requirements under the law), record keeping, and retention;
- the role and responsibilities of the compliance officer; and
- staff training.

Results of the reviews should be reported to the right person, including recommendations to rectify deficiencies identified.

Risk-Based Approach to Managing Risk

What is a risk-based approach?

NBFIs should be aware of the money laundering and terrorist financing risks that are implicit in their operations. These risks arise from a number of sources, including customers, products and services, delivery channels, and geographic regions and markets. Having understood the risks arising from doing business, NBFIs must develop sound risk management practices to assist them in managing risks posed by money laundering, terrorist financing, and other criminal activities.

What are the steps in risk-based approach?

A risk-based approach involves a number of discrete steps in ascertaining the most cost-effective and appropriate ways to manage and mitigate the risks of money laundering and terrorist financing faced by an NBFI. These steps are to identify the money laundering and terrorist financing risks that are pertinent to the NBFI in relation to its

- customers,
- products,
- delivery channels, and
- geographic areas of operation.

The steps are as follows:

1. Identify the risks.
2. Assess the risks.
3. Design and put in place controls to manage and reduce risks.
4. Monitor and improve the effective operation of the risk-based controls.

Risk identification

Identification is the first stage of the risk management process. NBFIs should be aware of the money laundering and terrorist financing risks that are implicit in their operations. NBFIs must be aware of and identify the types of money laundering and terrorist financing risks that arise from various sources.

NBFIs should also be aware of the money laundering and terrorist financing risks that exist in their jurisdiction in general. At a national level, this process requires the identification of risk factors associated with money laundering and terrorist financing threats and vulnerabilities. Threats are a function of the general levels of criminal and terrorist activity to which a country is exposed. Vulnerabilities are a function of political (the characteristics of the political system), economic (the nature of economic activity), social (demographic characteristics), technological (level of technological advancement), environmental (issues related to the physical environment), and legislative (the coverage, maturity, and effectiveness of the legislative system) factors.

Assessing the risk

The identification or recognition of risk is the first step in an effective risk management process. Beyond identifying risk, it is equally important to measure or quantify risk. Unless it is effectively measured, it is difficult to assess the potential impact that a given type or source of risk can have on an institution. NBFIs should therefore develop techniques and mechanisms that will allow them to assess the quantum of each type of money laundering and terrorist financing risk with which it is faced and the likely duration of such risk. If, for example, an NBFI considers a specific type of customer to represent a high money laundering or terrorist financing risk, then it should at all times be aware of the number of such customers it has and the types and volume of business activity and transactions they are conducting.

Managing the risk

Having identified and measured risks, NBFIs should develop a risk management framework and practices to effectively mitigate such risks. This requires the development of policies that reflect the institution's risk appetite and its approach to risk management, procedures that give effect to the policies, and limits that preclude undesirable levels of risk concentrations or exposures.

An important aspect of a framework for controlling risk is the establishment of clear lines of authority and reporting lines and responsibilities. Effective control of risk is also dependent on the institution's ability to communicate its policies, procedures, and limits to all employees and business units involved in the management of money laundering and terrorist financing risks.

NBFIs should establish effective systems for the ongoing monitoring of their risk exposures and the effectiveness of associated risk management systems and practices. NBFIs should therefore have management information system (MIS) that measures their inherent money laundering and terrorist financing risks and changes in such exposures. In the context of money laundering and terrorist financing risks, it is important, for example, that the MIS monitors the increase or decrease of the NBFI's exposure to such risk. The MIS should also, for example, monitor customer behavior and transactions to identify activity that may arouse suspicion of being linked to money laundering or terrorist financing.

Further, the MIS should monitor the adherence to established policies and procedures to determine, for example, when an established internal limit or legal and regulatory obligations have been breached. The MIS will also enable management to identify areas of concern or where risk management systems and practices need to be strengthened.

Benefits of a risk-based approach

A risk-based approach serves to balance the cost burden placed on the NBFI and its customers with a realistic assessment of the threat of the NBFI being used in money laundering or terrorist financing. A risk-based approach focuses the management of risk on those areas where it is needed and will have the greatest outcome.

To assist the overall objective of preventing money laundering and terrorist financing, a risk assessment form (example in Appendix 5) is to be completed by the compliance officer, providing clear reasoning for justification of the assigned risk category and due diligence, and is signed off by senior management on behalf of all customers and counterparts. This is completed for all new and high-risk customers and recognizes that the money laundering and terrorist financing threat to the NBFI varies across customers, products, geographic regions, and delivery channels.

This form assigns risk based on an assessment of customer, product, delivery channel, and geographic region which has been developed by the NBFI based on criteria outlined in the next section. Client relationships are assessed using this form and a risk score is calculated, and, on the basis of this score, the NBFI will monitor and manage the customer relationship. A high-risk customer relationship is subject to more intensive monitoring.

The risk-based strategy

The risk-based approach recognizes that a customer's profile can be determined at the start of the relationship. However, the profile of a customer's financial behavior, which allows the NBFI to identify transactions or activity that may be unusual or suspicious, will build up only over time.

The NBFI should adopt a categorization for risk assessment, for example, high, medium, or low. Criteria for each category to determine differing levels and treatments of client identification, verification, additional CDD (enhanced due diligence), information, and monitoring are for nonresident clients or transactions originating from other jurisdictions based on factors and/or information relating to that jurisdiction.

Information on nonresident jurisdiction is based on the Corruption Perception Index by Transparency International (as updated), together with the requisite guidance from the Financial Action Task Force and other agencies, such as the United Nations, the supervisory authority, and/or the financial intelligence unit. Such information is subject to regular review and at least annually by the compliance officer or staff of the compliance department or unit. The results are recorded for each customer and updated on the basis of risk.

The customer file and its related documented risk assessment should reflect the justification and reasoning of the assigned risk category, with clear recommendation(s) for the ongoing level of monitoring and the timeline for updating the risk assessment and due diligence details. The NBFI's identification program to reflect risk includes

- standard or enhanced information held with respect to all customers;
- standard or enhanced identification and verification requirements for all customers;
- enhanced due diligence (obtaining additional information on the customer, obtaining information on the source of funds or wealth of the customer, conducting enhanced monitoring of the business

relationship) for higher-risk customers, as determined by the risk assessment;

- where appropriate, reduced CDD requirements where the risk of money laundering or terrorist financing has been assessed as being low; and
- risk-based ongoing monitoring of customer activities and transactions that will enable the NBFI to ensure that transactions being conducted are consistent with the NBFI's knowledge of the customer. Customers assessed to be a higher risk will be subject to enhanced monitoring compared with customers assessed to be a low risk.

In addition, background information will be collected on high-risk customers; politically exposed persons (PEPs); individuals deemed high risk, geographically or otherwise; and companies and/or institutions that trade in or do business related to high-risk commodities.

This will also involve obtaining information to substantiate the source of wealth and funds of a high-risk customer.

Monitoring and improving the effective operation of risk-based controls

The effective management of risk is a continuous and dynamic process. The NBFI should ensure that the process for managing the risks of money laundering and terrorist financing is subject to regular review and is updated as new or emerging risks are identified.

Senior management should ensure that the NBFI keeps its risk assessment up to date. The review of the risk assessment, which should be conducted at least annually, will form part of the compliance officer's annual report to the institution's board and/or the senior management. In addition, to ensure that the NBFI's policies and procedures are being effectively implemented, a monitoring process should be put in place. The monitoring process will include

- ongoing monitoring of customer transactions, including ensuring that documents and information collected during the CDD process are kept up to date;

- keeping the NBFI's different products and services under review;
- reviewing the effectiveness of staff awareness and training;
- monitoring compliance arrangements through internal audit and external review;
- capturing appropriate management information;
- regular communication between the compliance officer and senior management; and
- liaising with law enforcement agencies.

Sources of risk

The risk assessment within each product and/or service area and the NBFI's own risk assessment is outlined below. However, as stated previously, when a product is provided to a higher-risk customer, the related risk will also automatically increase. Likewise, delivery of a product or service through a correspondent relationship may also increase the risk to the NBFI.

Senior management has classified retail banking, customer services, and personal and business accounts as follows:

Higher risk

- New accounts (opened other than on a non–face-to-face basis)
- Accounts operated under power of attorney
- Accounts of PEPs
- Accounts where a suspicious activity report has been made to the compliance officer
- Accounts where fraud has previously been attempted
- Accounts operated under trade finance activities
- Accounts operated through correspondent banking relationships
- Foreign exchange and money transfer services
- Occasional transactions for noncustomer
- Wire transfers
- Correspondent banking relationships

Medium risk

- Current accounts over 6 months old depending on the assigned risk category
- Accounts offering an overdraft facility

Lower risk

- Low-value foreign exchange activity and money transfer services
- Overdrafts and the provision of loan and credit facilities[2]

Managing delivery risk

International standards accept that there is a greater potential for money laundering or terrorist financing when the customer, or the customer's representative, has not been met on a face-to-face basis. Accounts opened or business relationships established other than on a face-to-face basis have been classified by the board and/or the senior management as presenting a higher level of risk depending on the nature of the customer.

Managing customer and geographical risk

The broad objective of the requirement to assess customer risk is to ensure that the NBFI knows its customers and understands the nature and purpose of the business relationship. The NBFI's knowledge and understanding of its customers and the type of transactions undertaken will increase over the life of the relationship. This will assist the NBFI to identify transactions which are not consistent with the NBFI's knowledge of the customer.

Usually, an NBFI has a range of personal, corporate, and business customers. Consequently, they have been classified as falling within a range of risks (high, medium, or low). Companies listed on regulated stock exchanges, governments, state-owned companies, and other regulated NBFIs may present a lower-level risk. PEPs, partnerships, sole traders, charities, and cash-intensive businesses present higher risks.

The identification of a customer as being high risk does not mean that the customer is involved in money laundering or the financing of terrorism. Similarly, the assessment of a customer as low risk does not mean that the customer is not involved. Risks related to dealing with customers need to be

---

[2] Overdrafts and loan and credit facilities are generally regarded as low risk; however, loan finance can be used by criminals to provide an air of normality and legitimacy to criminal transactions and operations. The main money-laundering risk arises through the early repayment of the loan.

understood. It is important that all employees understand and correctly apply the NBFI's risk-based approach when dealing with customers.

Corporate entities

Generally, any form of legal entity is a higher-risk customer. Companies may be owned wholly or partially by criminals with the objective of undertaking business based entirely on criminal funds and operations or, alternatively, with the objective of commingling legitimate and illegal business operations and funds.

Companies and structures presenting a higher level of risk

The risk increases with some private companies and structures, particularly those where the identity of the beneficial owner is obscure. Examples include

- companies that can be incorporated without the identity of the ultimate beneficial owners being known;
- companies that can be incorporated in one jurisdiction where they have no physical presence and operating in another jurisdiction;
- companies where a corporate service provider acts as the nominee of shareholders' and directors' companies issuing bearer shares; and
- corporate entities, for example, special purpose vehicles linked to trusts that can enhance the vulnerabilities.

Additional risks arise with companies operating in the following sectors:

- money services businesses (money exchangers and remitters),
- real estate, and
- dealers in high-value goods such as precious metals and stones.

To manage additional risks, in all cases, the company or partnership and its beneficial owners will be brought under the ambit of full CDD procedures, and additional CDD information will be obtained on the nature of the business undertaken.

Countries designated as higher-risk countries

The NBFI should be aware that shortcomings are evident in the AML/CFT legislation and standards. Additional advice on individual countries can be obtained, if necessary, from the compliance officer, who also has access to online resources and information from supervisory agencies and the financial intelligence unit.

In the event of the NBFI conducting a transaction with or from a high-risk jurisdiction, it will ensure that enhanced due diligence requirements are implemented to confirm that the NBFI understands the nature and purpose of the transaction(s).

In addition to internal assessments that identify high-risk jurisdictions, the NBFI will implement requirements as required by the supervisory agency and the financial intelligence unit in relation to countries that have been designated as high-risk countries. The compliance officer will ensure that all measures as required by the supervisory agency and the financial intelligence unit are implemented and, if required, suspicious transaction reports are submitted to the financial intelligence unit.

Enhanced due diligence and monitoring of higher-risk accounts

Enhanced due diligence and enhanced account monitoring procedures should be put in place to oversee accounts that are considered to be high risk, such as accounts of PEPs, correspondent banking accounts, and those related to trade finance.

Enhanced due diligence

The NBFI should apply enhanced due diligence measures where it has determined that the risk of money laundering or the financing of terrorism has been assessed as high. The compliance officer should have adequate oversight of all high-risk relationships (including non–face-to-face accounts, accounts of PEPs, and accounts related to correspondent banking and trade finance business).

The NBFI must keep copies of the customer's identity documentation, risk assessments and updated risk assessments, and other CDD information as specified by law and for the minimum period specified by law after the termination of the business relationship, as well as transactional documents for a minimum period as specified by law after the completion of the transaction.

Managing the risk of terrorist financing

The controls the NBFI has in place in relation to terrorism will be the same as the AML measures covering risk assessment, CDD checks, transaction monitoring, screening processes, reporting suspicious transactions, and liaising with supervisory authorities and the financial intelligence unit. The compliance officer is responsible for identifying sources of information of terrorist financing risks (e.g., press reports, information from supervisory authorities, the financial intelligence unit, Financial Action Task Force typologies, and court judgments).

Terrorism contrasts with those involved in the laundering of money where financial gain is the objective. However, terrorist organizations that operate either on a global or national scale use banking and money transfer facilities to launder their funds and facilitate terrorist activities.

Terrorists use money to carry out their activities and achieve their goals. For this, they need to use the financial institutions. A terrorist organization therefore develops funding sources and ensures that sources and uses of those funds are obscured. It also finds ways to make sure that the funds are available to enable it to commit terrorist acts.

Checking against sanctions lists
(sanctions and asset freezes)

Senior management should know the NBFI's obligations regarding sanctions imposed on persons designated as terrorists or involved in terrorist financing. The compliance officer is responsible for ensuring that customers are screened against lists of persons designated as terrorists or involved in the financing of terrorism and that, where potential matches are identified, appropriate actions are implemented as specified by law in a timely manner.

To ensure that the NBFI is not used by terrorists or those seeking to finance terrorism, the NBFI must check the lists issued through United Nations Security Council resolutions and information from the financial intelligence unit or the supervisory authority. If the NBFI fails to monitor these notices and checks customers against these lists, it runs the risk of breaching international sanctions legislation. The NBFI must adhere to any specific prohibition notices or any other advisories relating to the country of operation.

Awareness Raising and Training of the Staff

Statutory requirements

The effectiveness of the NBFI's AML and counterterrorist financing procedures depends on how well the NBFI's staff understand their responsibilities and the serious nature of money laundering and terrorist financing.

One of the most important controls over the prevention and detection of money laundering and terrorist financing is to have staff who understand these risks. Staff must be well-trained to identify activities or transactions that may be related to money laundering or the financing of terrorism. The staff who meet with customers or handle transactions and instructions are the NBFI's strongest defense against money laundering and terrorist financing.

To comply with the law, the staff must be made aware of the obligations placed on them and the NBFI under the law. This includes the requirement that staff are trained on how to recognize and deal with transactions and other activity(ies) that might be related to money laundering and terrorist financing.

Consequently, the NBFI will implement steps to ensure that all pertinent staff are aware of

- the laws relating to money laundering and terrorist financing;
- the risks that money laundering and terrorist financing pose to the NBFI, its business(es), and the jurisdiction;
- how the NBFI's products and services may be used as a vehicle to launder money or finance terrorism, and the NBFI's procedures for dealing with these risks;
- the risks posed by high-risk customers;
- the NBFI's policies and procedures for preventing money laundering and terrorist financing, and its risk assessment strategy;
- the identity and responsibilities of the compliance officer; and
- the consequences for them and for the NBFI if they fail to implement the NBFI's procedures.

Regulatory obligations

The law requires a commitment to provide staff training in relation to money laundering and terrorist financing to ensure that

- employees are competent,
- employees are supervised and understand their obligations,
- employees' performance is reviewed regularly, and
- the level of staff competence is appropriate to the nature of their job and of the business.

Awareness raising

All staff should be informed of their responsibilities and those of the NBFI at the commencement of their employment, and of the statutory obligations under which the NBFI operates and under which the employees could be held personally liable for failing to comply with these requirements.

All pertinent staff, whether permanent or temporary, should be made aware of the importance of the contents of their institution's policy and procedures handbook, especially the CDD requirements for preventing money laundering and terrorist financing. This includes the relevance of customer identification procedures, the need to obtain additional CDD information, and the need to monitor customer activity(ies).

The NBFI should be committed to providing staff with adequate training and awareness within the AML prevention training regime, as well as to ensuring that the staff are aware of their legal obligations and personal responsibilities in preventing money laundering and terrorist financing. The training should be given to enable the staff to recognize a transaction that is unusual or suspicious against the customer's profile. The training should also address terrorist funding and terrorist activity(ies) to ensure that the staff can identify customer transactions or activity(ies) that might be related to terrorism.

Ongoing training

The NBFI should provide ongoing training to all relevant staff at regular intervals. The methods of training should vary depending on the perceived need. Training should be face-to-face seminars or workshops and through refresher computer-based learning. As money-laundering risks differ depending on the particular nature of the product or service and the method of delivery, the training should be tailored to reflect the duties of the pertinent staff.

To ensure that the NBFI can provide evidence that statutory requirements have been met, the compliance officer should retain records setting out

- when training was given;
- the subject material;
- details of staff who attended the training; and
- test results, if applicable, that staff were required to complete.

Figure 2: Sources of "Dirty" Money to Be Laundered

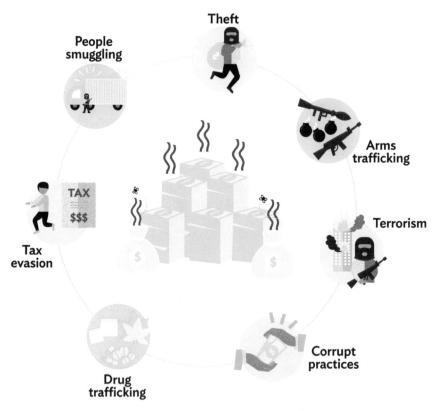

Source: AUSTRAC.

Part B
PROCEDURES

Policies and procedures set out the day-to-day measures that should be employed to ensure that the nonbank financial institution (NBFI) effectively identifies, measures, monitors, and controls money laundering and financing of terrorism risks. They should therefore

- be developed to reflect the risks implicit in an institution's customers, products and services, delivery channels, and geographic regions;
- be comprehensively documented and communicated to all staff;
- be subject to periodic review to ensure they are appropriate in light of changes to the institution's money laundering and terrorist financing risk profile; and
- clearly set out lines of responsibility and accountability for the execution of the risk management function and also establish effective reporting lines for all persons and business units involved in the management of money laundering and terrorist financing risks.

Customer Due Diligence Requirements

International standards outline minimum customer due diligence (CDD) requirements which include

- identifying and verifying the identity of the customer;
- identifying and verifying, on a risk-based approach, the beneficial owner and any other third parties involved in the relationship, wherein the customer is not the beneficial owner of the funds or assets to be used in the transaction, and where the beneficial owner owns or controls 25% or more of the company;
- understanding the ownership and corporate structure of the customer, where the customer is a company, a complex structure, or any other legal entity, for example, a trust or charity;
- getting information on the purpose and nature of the business relationship; and
- keeping all CDD information up to date and monitoring the account and relationship against the expected profile.

The NBFI will conduct regular checks by reviewing customer names against databases to ensure that its customers' names are not included on any sanctions list, such as those circulated by the financial intelligence unit, the supervisory authority, or the United Nations. Such checks will be conducted only on a monthly basis, unless the staff have reasons to suspect that the customer may be involved in money laundering, criminal, or terrorism-related activities.

The NBFI will not open an account or establish a relationship with a customer who gives a false and/or fictitious name.

All prospective customers will be risk-assessed for money laundering and terrorist financing purposes at the start of the relationship and the assessment will be kept under review. Additional due diligence will be applied to accounts and relationships where there is a greater potential for money laundering and terrorist financing. Ongoing CDD and monitoring procedures will be determined on the basis of risk.

Account opening policies

The NBFI should only deal with reputable customers who are engaged in legitimate personal or business activities. New customers that do not appear to be genuine must be declined, particularly those applicants who do not supply proof of identity and address or meet the NBFI's customer acceptance requirements.

Signing off new accounts

No accounts should be permitted to operate, even for the initial receipt of funds to open them, until all of the requirements have been completed to the satisfaction of the department manager and the compliance officer.

The prime responsibility for completing the account opening process rests with an account officer, starting with interviewing the customer personally, completing the documentation, obtaining the approval, opening a customer file, and finishing the account opening process. The compliance officer and senior department staff of the relevant business unit will ensure that all procedures have been completed and that all identification and other relevant

documents have been checked to ensure their validity and completeness, with respect to the following:

- The account opening form is correctly completed and signed.
- The passport and the driver's license (including photograph) are valid.
- Identity cards for foreign nationals are in compliance with the NBFI's requirements.
- Identification documents seen are originals and not copies.
- All documents provided relate to the applicant.

This handbook also includes checklist for the account opening for individuals (Appendix 6) and businesses (Appendix 7).

Requirements for Establishing a Relationship or Opening an Account

- The NBFI's standard account opening forms must be used in all cases. All forms held must be originals, completed in full, and signed. Facsimiles or photocopies are not acceptable.
- Evidence of identification must be obtained from all applicants even where a member of the staff or the management, another respected customer, or another group entity makes the introduction.
- As no single form of identification can give sufficient assurance that a customer is genuine, the identification process will be cumulative. A person's address is a key requirement and therefore verification of the customer's address is a requirement, in addition to the verification of the customer's name and/or identity.
- With respect to joint personal account holders, the identity of each applicant must be verified.
- Where funds being deposited are supplied by, or on behalf of, a third person, the identity of that person must also be established and verified.

- Identification documents seen must be originals. Certified file copies must be placed on the customer file and records of the supporting documents must be retained for 5 years after closure of the account. Certified copies of documentary evidence used to verify the identity and address must be stamped "originals seen by the NBFI and signed and dated."
- Where personal documentary evidence includes a photograph, the certification should be extended to confirm that the photograph is a true likeness of the customer. Staff should ensure that the customer can be identified from the copy of the photograph.
- For corporate customers, the requirement is to identify not only the company itself but also to verify its principal owners and controllers. In such cases, the NBFI should obtain the same information on principal owners and controllers as it would for an individual customer.

Identifying third parties

Where the customer informs the NBFI that funds to be deposited come from another party or the transaction is being conducted on behalf of another person, the identity of that person must also be established and verified.

The underlying beneficial owner of the funds being deposited or invested may not be the account holder in all cases. If funds being deposited are supplied by, or on behalf of, a third party, or the account is to be operated, managed, or controlled by a third party, the identity of this party must also be established and verified. The identification requirements applied to third parties are the same as those applied to individuals seeking to open a new account or establish a business relationship.

New account applications for previous customers

New accounts opened or reactivated for previous customers will be treated as new relationships and the appropriate account opening form, together with the full documentary evidence of name and permanent address, must be obtained, even in circumstances where the customer retains the previous account number. The new account records must be cross-referenced to the previous account(s).

New accounts for existing customers

In cases where an existing customer closes one type of account but opens another type of account, there is no need to conduct additional CDD. However, in such circumstances, staff should take the opportunity to reconfirm existing CDD details on the customer to incorporate any new details and to obtain any missing information. Where there has been significant change in the customer details since the original relationship was established or where any doubt exists as to the veracity of that original documentation, the customer's identity should be reverified.

Financial sanctions

The monitoring and screening of individuals and entities as identified on the relevant lists, advised to the NBFI, are important, as the law, in the case of a terrorist, requires NBFIs not to provide funds or financial services to persons on sanctions lists. These lists, which are maintained by the compliance officer, include the following:

- United Nations Security Council resolutions relating to the Taliban and other terrorist groups or persons;
- countries identified by the Financial Action Task Force as having deficient anti-money laundering and combating the financing of terrorism (AML/CFT) frameworks and where the Financial Action Task Force has called upon member countries to impose countermeasures;
- countries identified by the financial intelligence unit or the supervisory authority as having deficient AML/CFT frameworks; and
- countries that the NBFI has identified as having deficient AML/CFT frameworks.

The compliance department receives daily urgent and updated sanction notices distributed by the authorities, which are reviewed and passed onto each department for review against their customer base, clients, and countries of trade. As part of daily duties, the compliance officer or department will review details of transactions (customer name and/or beneficiary) conducted by or through the NBFI against the lists received.

The immediate point of contact for any financial sanctions issues is the compliance officer.

Prior to account opening, following completion of the customer file, and before providing or undertaking any transactions for a prospective customer, the staff are required to check customer information (including that of the beneficiary in the case of funds transfer) against lists maintained by the compliance officer and other public information (such as the internet). The compliance officer should conduct further screening through global screening, which will also include directors, beneficial owners, and, where adequate information is available, third-party payees.

On a daily basis, the staff are required to check details of customer transactions (including beneficiaries of funds transfers) against the lists received from authorities, which are kept up to date by the compliance officer. Where a match is identified, the compliance officer shall be informed immediately. The compliance officer will review information on the customer and transaction, and where

    i.   it is determined that there is no match:
- inform the staff to process the transaction(s). In the event that uncertainty remains as to the identification of the customer, the compliance officer shall contact the financial intelligence unit to obtain additional information on the customer; or

    ii.   it is determined that there is a match:
- immediately inform the financial intelligence unit by submitting a suspicious transaction report,
- instruct the staff to freeze the account and suspend all transactions, and
- pass the administration of account or relationship immediately to the compliance officer and/or senior management.

Account opening for personal customers

To confirm the identity of customers, the following information should be obtained from new customers seeking to open an account with the NBFI:

- true name and/or names used,
- passport or other official identification document (current and with a photograph of the customer),

- current permanent address,
- date of birth, and
- nationality.

Other transactions for personal customers

Information to be obtained from customers seeking to conduct a transaction through the NBFI:

- true name and/or names used,
- passport or other official identification document (current and with a photograph of the customer),
- current permanent address,
- date of birth,
- nationality, and
- source of funds.

Foreign resident personal customers

A current signed passport is required as personal evidence of identity for prospective nonresident customers. Certified copies confirming that the photograph represents a true likeness must be taken for the NBFI's records in all cases.

The current permanent address of the prospective customer must also be verified through one of the following means:

- sighting of a recent (i.e., up to 3 months old) original utility bill;
- sighting of a certified copy of an original statement, not older than 3 months, from a financial institution in the customer's home jurisdiction; or
- sighting of an original tax notification.

In addition, where considered necessary, but not as a substitute for the procedures listed above, confirmation should be sought from a financial institution, which the NBFI has determined to have good AML/CFT controls, in the customer's country of origin verifying the customer's true name, residential address, date of birth, nationality, and signature.

Other types of personal or individual accounts offered

As appropriate, the NBFI should develop procedures for the opening of other types of accounts it offers to different types of customers (e.g., youth saver accounts). CDD requirements should be consistent with those outlined earlier for individual customers.

Politically exposed persons

All such accounts and relationships, including where a politically exposed person (PEP) is the customer or beneficial owner, are classified as higher risk, and in addition to completing the account opening procedures and standard CDD identification checks, inquiries will be made to establish the source of wealth and the source of funds to be used in the relationship.

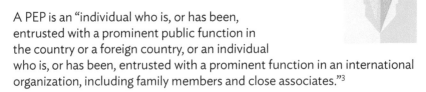

A PEP is an "individual who is, or has been, entrusted with a prominent public function in the country or a foreign country, or an individual who is, or has been, entrusted with a prominent function in an international organization, including family members and close associates."[3]

Documents required are as follows:

- passport (certified);
- proof of address, e.g., utility bill (not more than 3 months old);
- statement of source of wealth; and
- media articles on the customer.

Information is collected on the following:

- reason for opening the account,
- expected use of the account, and
- information on associates of the customer with whom he or she is likely to do business or otherwise.

---

[3] Financial Action Task Force. 2012. *International Standards on Combating Money Laundering and the Financing of Terrorism and Proliferation*. Paris.

Furthermore, all individual PEP account opening requests should be conducted on a face-to-face basis, where proof of identity and signature can be verified.

Inquiries regarding the reputation of the PEP or related individual(s) should include the following:

i. Consultation with the senior manager or the correspondent business manager of a financial institution in the home country of the PEP or related individual(s).

ii. A review of generally available public information regarding the PEP or related individuals, such as news articles from reputable sources.

iii. Enhanced due diligence, monitoring of all transactions over the account on a daily basis, utilizing screening processes.

iv. Intraday transactions scrutinized and reviewed on a monthly basis.

v. Background information on the client and the client's associates, including internet and media news articles.

vi. Full screening check against all sanctions lists and crime lists, scrutiny of passport information, and media checks.

vii. Statement of source of wealth from the prospective customer. Evidence to back this should be sought. If this evidence is provided by the customer, then substantiation of this evidence should be sought, including use of the internet or confirmation from an accountant and/or auditor.

For customers who are categorized as PEPs, as part of the enhanced due diligence process, the accounts are subject to an additional review every month, the results of which are recorded in the customer file and signed off by the compliance officer and the senior management.

For opening of new accounts for PEPs from foreign countries, or where there are concerns about the domestic/international PEP, prior approval of the general manager is required. The operation of the account will be kept under review by the compliance officer.

Account opening for registered and private companies

The following information must be obtained for all registered companies prior to opening the account:

- full legal name;
- registered company number, if applicable;
- registered office address in the country of incorporation;
- business address;
- nature of the company's business; and
- completion of the account opening form.

Documents required to evidence the company are

- certificate of incorporation;
- board resolution or mandate to open an account;
- memorandum of articles and association;
- registration of address;
- company structure;
- ultimate ownership and beneficial ownership;
- names of all directors, controllers, and signatories; and
- latest audited accounts (otherwise management accounts; for new companies, financial projections should be sought).

For private companies and unincorporated businesses:

- certified certificate of incorporation;
- names of beneficial owners holding over 25% of the shares;[4]
- completed beneficial owners holding over 25% of the shares;[5]
- source of wealth statement for PEPs and beneficial owners;
- identification of controllers and/or directors, and signatories (i.e., passports and proof of address); and
- certified list of signatures.

[4] Subject to change to reflect jurisdiction requirements.
[5] Footnote 4.

Verifying the identity of beneficial owners and controllers of private companies and businesses

The level of satisfaction concerning the identity of beneficial owners will depend on the level of risk involved. In general, private companies, will require greater information, including verification of identity and address for

i. the principal underlying beneficial owner(s)—normally those holding 25% or more;[6] however, a flexible approach must be adopted to ensure verification of all shareholders capable of exercising control and direction over the company, either individually or in tandem;
ii. persons with principal control over the company's assets, e.g., principal controllers and/or directors, and shadow directors (i.e., those with power to issue instructions to the company); and
iii. other significant directors and signatories.

Each beneficial owner or controller should provide the appropriate documents as required for individual or corporate customers. Where the beneficial owner or the controller of a company is another company or legal entity, then proof of the ultimate beneficial owner of that company or legal entity should be obtained.

Account opening for other types of legal persons (e.g., trusts and nonprofit organizations)

As appropriate, the NBFI should develop procedures for the opening of other types of accounts it offers to types of legal persons and arrangements. CDD requirements should be consistent with those for companies as outlined above. In the case of trusts and charities, such procedures should also include

i. trusts: the identity of settlor,[7] the trustees, the beneficiaries or class of beneficiaries, and any other natural person exercising ultimate effective control over the trust (including through a chain of control and/or ownership); and
ii. nonprofit organizations: the purpose and objectives of the organization, the identity of persons exercising control, senior officers (such as board members), and the source and use of funds.

---

[6] Footnote 4.
[7] The natural or legal persons who transfer ownership of their assets to the trustees by means of a trust deed or similar arrangement.

Correspondent banking relationships

Prior to opening an account with a correspondent financial institution, the following information should be obtained:

- full legal name;
- company registration number, if applicable;
- registered office in the country of incorporation;
- business address;
- nature of the institution's business, including information on customers;
- latest statement of accounts; and
- the nature of the relationship and the types of transactions to be conducted through the account.

In addition, the NBFI must seek and assess information relating to the supervisory framework under which the institution operates, the AML/CFT framework in the institution's home jurisdiction, the institution's own AML/CFT policies and procedures, and whether the institution has been subject to any actions imposed by supervisory or other authorities in relation to money laundering or the financing of terrorism.

The relationship must be established only with prior approval of the senior management.

When identification cannot be completed

In circumstances where a customer is unwilling or unable to provide all required CDD information, the relationship or request to open an account will be declined. In some cases, where a customer is unable or unwilling to provide required information or documentation and provides no valid explanation, staff should prepare and submit a suspicious transaction report to the compliance officer. The compliance officer will review the report and consider submitting it to the financial intelligence unit.

Wire transfers and other remittances

Full details of all remittances, as required by law, must be recorded. The names of the beneficiary must also be recorded. If information as required by law relating to the name of the originator (including details of the transaction) is

not provided by the customer, then the transaction will not be processed and the NBFI will consider submitting a report to the financial intelligence unit.

If staff have any concerns about the validity of the documents provided by the customer, reference must be made to senior management and/or the compliance officer before conducting the transaction. Copies of supporting documents must be kept together with the wire transfer application form.

In circumstances where the NBFI's knowledge of the customer is not consistent with the value or purpose of the remittance but staff are satisfied regarding the explanation given for the remittance, the remittance may be processed for payment. Future requests to transfer funds should be monitored against the customer profile to confirm or deny the initial explanation. Should staff form a view that the customer may be involved in money laundering or terrorist financing, a suspicious transaction report must be completed and submitted to the compliance officer.

Inward remittances

Payment of cash in excess of the threshold amount, if applicable, to non-account holders through the NBFI will require evidence of the remitter's name, address, and account number or unique identification number. An explanation for the source of the funds and their purpose should also be obtained. If the funds are to be collected by the beneficiary, then evidence of proof of identity of the beneficiary should also be provided.

Where inward remittances are received that do not include the required information as specified by law, the NBFI should approach the remitting bank to obtain missing information. If the information is not provided, the NBFI may, depending on the size and nature of the transaction, accept the payment and provide funds to the beneficiary, decline to accept the funds and return the funds to the sending institution, or, through the compliance officer, submit a report to the financial intelligence unit.

Dormant accounts

Reactivation of dormant accounts can only be undertaken following reverification of the account holder in line with the requirements for new customers.

Reviewing Customer Due Diligence Information and Monitoring Customer Accounts

The requirement to monitor customer activity

The law requires the NBFI to conduct ongoing monitoring of their customer relationships, including

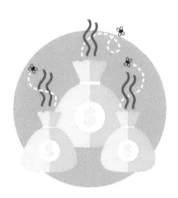

- scrutinizing transactions throughout the relationship to ensure that these are consistent with the customer's business activities and risk profile; and
- ensuring that documents, data, and other information relating to the customer are kept up to date.

Monitoring and updating will permit the customer's risk assessment to be kept up to date and enable the NBFI to establish a pattern of transactions.

Monitoring recently opened accounts

On the basis of the risk assessment performed, recently opened accounts, where the NBFI is yet to fully determine the nature and purpose of transactions, should be subject to increased monitoring. As part of the standard procedure, newly opened accounts will be managed and overseen in order to verify whether the activities and details advised during the account opening process are consistent with expectations

- to establish a normal pattern of transactions;
- to ensure that transactions are consistent with the customer's expected business activity established during account opening;
- to ensure that the verified CDD information provided when the account/relationship was established remains unchanged (e.g., no change of name, address, or account signatories);
- to ascertain and record, if appropriate, CDD information on the beneficial owner and source of funds in the account and verify

the identity of any third party in accordance with jurisdiction requirements; and

- to ensure that transactions are consistent with the NBFI's knowledge of the customer's business.

Updating knowledge of the customer

The expected activity, based on information obtained from the customer when the account and/or relationship was established, of all customer accounts must be kept up to date by all relevant staff, with particular reference to

- documenting customer transactions,
- documenting events that are considered important to give the NBFI a better understanding of the customer and their activities,
- large cash transactions being undertaken,
- providing the compliance officer with customer and CDD information, and
- making sure that the NBFI knows the identity of the beneficial owner of funds.

Documentation to be held in customer files should include notes and reports containing details of

- the customer, reason for opening the account(s) with the NBFI, any beneficial owner, third party, etc.; and
- the nature of the customer's business, including seasonal trends, expected volume of transactions, etc.

In ensuring that customer information is kept up to date, a file note (including call reports) as and when appropriate must be completed by staff. Such notes should record meetings and telephone discussions with the customer.

The following specific trigger events will give rise to a full review of the CDD information and documentation for a corporate or business client:

- change of ownership,
- change in the nature of the business,
- significant increase in turnover, and
- noticeable changes in the nature of transactions or activity(ies).

Undertaking a risk-based review

All accounts should undergo a general review of customer and enhanced due diligence information, with the timing of the review being determined by their risk rating. Higher-risk accounts will be reviewed at least annually with lower-risk accounts being reviewed less frequently.

The risk review should either confirm that the original risk assessment is relevant or should indicate where that assessment is no longer correct. The reasons for the change should also be recorded.

Monitoring transactions and activity(ies)

The most important safeguard against money laundering and terrorist financing is ongoing monitoring of customers and transactions as it could identify suspicious activities and enable the NBFI to take further action to prevent recurrence of such activity(ies). Therefore, managers and department managers should monitor all activity(ies) on an ongoing basis to ensure that

- transactions being conducted are consistent with the NBFI's knowledge of the customer, and
- all relevant information has been taken into account to assess whether the customer has conducted transactions which could be related to money laundering or the financing of terrorism.

Reviews of activity will be written and retained as required under the NBFI's record-keeping policy.

Cash transactions for account holders

Cash transactions, particularly large cash transactions, present a risk to the NBFI as there is little or no supporting information to substantiate the source of funds. Accordingly, transactions involving cash should be subject to additional scrutiny especially in cases where the transaction is not consistent with the NBFI's knowledge of the customer. Any questionable activity must be examined to establish the source of funds and/or wealth, if appropriate, and to determine and document the reason for the cash transaction. Third parties depositing cash into customer accounts should be asked to provide documentary evidence of their link to the account holder.

Managers and department managers should be aware of those customers whose businesses are cash intensive (e.g., retail outlets or restaurants), and this information should be included in the customer profile. The NBFI should, based on discussions with the customer, understand the expected size and frequency of cash deposits made by customers. Cash transactions should be reasonable for the customer's business, based on knowledge of the customer, and cash transactions which appear inconsistent with the NBFI's knowledge of the customer should be subject to review. In addition, large and frequent foreign currency cash transactions, are potentially suspicious particularly if these are inconsistent with the customer's business activities.

If on a single day the established cash limit is exceeded, or if there is no such limit and cash transactions exceed the legal threshold or its equivalent, then the staff should review the transactions at the end of the day to confirm that no suspicious activity is involved.

Cash transactions conducted by customers that exceed the legislated threshold are to be reported to the financial intelligence unit.

Monitoring wire transfer remittances

The NBFI should ensure that inward wire transfers are compliant with the legislated information requirements. However, in order not to disrupt straight-through processing, monitoring is not expected to be done at the time of processing the transfer.

Where information on inward payments does not meet the requirements of the law, the NBFI should seek additional information from the remitting bank and/or institution. In the event such additional information is not available or forthcoming, the NBFI should, on the basis of the risk, return the funds to the sending institution, make a payment to the beneficiary, or submit a report to the financial intelligence unit.

Review of inward and outward remittances for account holders

A daily review should be undertaken by the appropriate officer to ensure that the information on the frequency and size of the remittances, their points of origin and destination, and their originators are consistent with the NBFI's knowledge of the customer. Any suspicions should be reported promptly to the compliance officer.

Recognizing Suspicious Activity

What is suspicion?

As money launderers or persons involved in terrorist financing can use various types of transactions, it is difficult to define a suspicious transaction or activity. Suspicion is personal and subjective depending on a range of factors and falls far short of proof. However, staff should have some basis for determining if a transaction or activity is suspicious and it is therefore important that staff receive adequate training to assist them to identify suspicious transactions or activity.

A suspicious activity or transaction may be

- any transaction or instruction that is not logical from an economic or financial point of view, and
- any transaction that is inconsistent with the NBFI's knowledge of the customer or expected account activity(ies).

Recognizing suspicions

The process of recognizing suspicions has three components:

i.   Having sufficient knowledge about a customer's normal expected activity.
ii. With enough knowledge, being able to distinguish the abnormal or unusual from the normal or usual.
iii. As a result, being able to then recognize what might be suspicious.

Examples of suspicious transactions are provided in Appendix 8.

Notification and reporting of suspected fraud or other criminal activity(ies)

Any member of the staff or the management who discovers or suspects fraudulent or other criminal activity(ies), including terrorist financing, must contact the compliance officer and complete a suspicious transaction report. Failure to report a reasonably grounded suspicion, or reckless disregard of signs that should raise a suspicion, will be regarded as a disciplinary offense and could constitute a criminal offense.

Any employee who reports a suspicion or is otherwise aware that an investigation is being, or may be, conducted must take particular care at all times to avoid committing a tipping-off offense, that is, informing the customer or other parties that a report of suspicion has been provided to the compliance officer.

Duty to report and investigate suspicions of money laundering or terrorist financing

- It is the duty of every employee to report any suspicious transaction(s) or activity(ies) to the compliance officer. Reporting should be done using the reporting procedures set out in this section.
- All internal reports must reach the compliance officer and must not be blocked at the department level.
- The compliance officer should investigate the report. He or she should review all available information, including reviewing past transaction history and CDD information and make additional inquiries to determine whether the transaction or instruction is consistent with the NBFI's knowledge of the customer or if additional information obtained from the customer can be relied upon to decide that the transaction or instruction is not suspicious.
- The compliance officer must, on request, be provided with all information relating to any of the customers to enable him or her to assess a report and to determine whether there is any information in the NBFI's possession that would remove the suspicion.
- Where the compliance officer, on the basis of further investigations, determines that the suspicious transaction report prepared by staff is justified, the report should be submitted to the financial intelligence unit, as required by the law. In making this determination, the compliance officer should not require the approval of any other persons in the NBFI.

Procedures for reporting suspicions

Staff with any suspicion of money laundering or terrorist financing must report it immediately to the compliance officer using the approved suspicious transaction report form.

In the event of a potential financial sanctions target match that clearly identifies a name or entity as suspicious, the compliance officer should be immediately notified. The transaction should not be completed unless approval has been received.

How to behave when faced with an abnormal or suspicious transaction or activity

A member of the staff faced with a customer, transaction, or situation that he or she feels is suspicious must

- immediately seek the advice of the department manager who will decide whether to accept the transaction or whether to immediately submit the details to the compliance officer to enable him or her to take a decision;
- as far as technically possible, delay execution of the transaction to enable a decision to be made;
- take note of all information available on the proposed transaction, and photocopy documents submitted, if possible;
- never mention in any manner whatsoever the actual reason for the delay or reluctance to execute the transaction requested;
- remain evasive about the internal decision-making procedures, with respect to the transaction in question; and
- not recontact the customer, except where necessary to protect the interests of the NBFI, or in exceptional circumstances, and that too as per the direction of the compliance officer.

Compliance officer procedures

When the compliance officer receives a suspicious transaction report, he or she will log it, allocate a reference number, and acknowledge receipt. He or she will then undertake sufficient inquiries to determine whether, in his or her judgment, the concerned transaction is suspicious. This action must be undertaken promptly.

The compliance officer may review

- the account opening records and CDD and other information obtained from the customer,
- historical transaction patterns, and
- any previous suspicious transaction reports.

The compliance officer may discuss the report with

- the members of the staff and/or the senior management, or
- other members of the management, as appropriate.

The compliance officer must

- document his or her inquiries and the reason for deciding to/not to forward the suspicious transaction report to the financial intelligence unit.

Record Keeping

Document retention

The records prepared and maintained by the NBFI must be such that

- the requirements of the law and expectations of the regulator or the supervisor are fully met;[8]
- auditors, reporting accountants, and regulators or supervisors are able to assess the effectiveness of NBFI's AML/CFT policies and procedures;
- any transaction or instruction conducted through the NBFI on behalf of any individual customer can be reconstructed;
- any customer or underlying beneficial owner can be properly identified;
- all suspicious transaction reports received internally, and those submitted to the financial intelligence unit, can be identified; and
- the NBFI can meet, within the required time frame, any inquiries or court orders from the appropriate law enforcement agencies.

---

[8] Subject to the jurisdiction's law.

How long should records be retained?

The minimum periods for which records must be maintained to comply with the requirements of the law are outlined in the following table:[9]

Type of Account	Length of Retention
Account opening records and documentary evidence of identity	At least 5 years after account closure
Account ledger records	At least 5 years
Individual transaction records	At least 5 years
Results of any analysis undertaken (e.g., inquiries to establish the background and purpose of complex, usual large transactions)	At least 5 years after account closure
Information after the account has been closed or after the last transaction	At least 5 years

Source: Financial Action Task Force.

Records relating to a customer's identity must be retained for at least 5 years from the date of closure of business with the client.[10] The date on which the relationship with a customer ends is the date of

- carrying out a one-off transaction or the last in the series of transactions; or
- ending of the business relationship, that is, the closing of an account.

[9]   Footnote 8.
[10] Footnote 8.

Glossary

Money laundering is the process by which illegally obtained funds, or cash or property derived from criminal activities, are given a semblance of legality. In other words, it is a process meant to clean "dirty" money to disguise its criminal origin.

Terrorist financing, or financing of terrorism, refers to the processing of funds to sponsor or facilitate terrorist activity.

Beneficial owner(s) refers to the natural person(s) who ultimately owns or controls a customer and/or the natural person on whose behalf a transaction is being conducted. It also includes those persons who exercise ultimate effective control over a legal person or arrangement.

Beneficiary refers to the natural or legal person or legal arrangement that is identified by the originator as the receiver of the requested wire transfer.

Financial Action Task Force (FATF) is the international standard setter in the fight against money laundering and terrorist financing. The standards are known as the FATF 40 Recommendations and were last updated in 2012.

Cross-border wire transfer refers to any wire transfer (or telegraphic transfer) where the ordering financial institution and the beneficiary financial institution are located in different countries. This term also refers to any chain of wire transfers in which at least one of the financial institutions involved is located in a different country.

Originator refers to the account holder who allows the wire transfer from that account or, where there is no account, the natural or legal person that places the order with the ordering financial institution to perform the wire transfer.

Correspondent banking is the provision of banking services by one bank (the correspondent bank) to another bank (the respondent bank). Large international banks typically act as correspondents for thousands of other banks around the world. Respondent banks may be provided with a wide range

of services, including cash management (e.g., interest-bearing accounts in a variety of currencies), international wire transfers, and check clearing, payable-through accounts and foreign exchange services.

Legal persons refer to any entities other than natural persons that can establish a permanent customer relationship with the institution or otherwise own property. This can include companies, bodies corporate, foundations, partnerships, or associations and other similar entities.

Politically exposed persons (PEPs) can refer to (i) *domestic PEPs*: individuals who are, or have been, entrusted domestically with prominent public functions (e.g., heads of state or of government; senior politicians; senior government, judicial, or military officials; senior executives of state-owned corporations; important political party officials; and any other stated by law); (ii) *foreign PEPs*: individuals who are, or have been, entrusted with prominent public functions by a foreign country (e.g., heads of state or of government; senior politicians; senior government, judicial, or military officials; senior executives of state-owned corporations; and important political party officials); or (iii) *international PEPs*: individuals who are, or have been, entrusted with a prominent function by an international organization and are members of senior management (i.e., directors, deputy directors, and members of the board or equivalent functionaries).

This term also includes family members as well as individuals who are related to the PEP, either directly or through marriage or similar (civil) forms of relationship, and close associates of PEPs who are individuals connected with the PEP either socially or professionally.

Responsibilities and Roles of Directors and Senior Management

Minimum requirements

Directors and senior managers must

- undertake a risk assessment which identifies the vulnerability of the nonbank financial institution (NBFI) to be used to launder money or finance terrorists;
- on the basis of the risk assessment, implement a risk management framework to ensure that the NBFI is not used to launder money or finance terrorists;
- ensure that the risk management framework is risk based with sufficient resources being devoted to dealing with higher-risk customers and transactions;
- ensure that the NBFI has appropriate compliance management arrangements, including the appointment of a compliance officer at management level; and
- devote sufficient resources to deal with money laundering and terrorist financing, including ensuring that the compliance function is adequately resourced and that staff receive appropriate and adequate training.

Actions required

Senior managers must

- carry out a risk assessment, which should be reviewed and updated on a regular basis, identifying where the business is vulnerable to money laundering and terrorist financing;
- based on the risk assessment, develop internal policies, procedures, and controls to combat money laundering and the financing of terrorism;

- ensure staff effectively implement the internal policies, procedures, and controls and receive appropriate training; and
- monitor the implementation of the NBFI's policies, procedures, and controls and make improvements where required on the basis of changes to the NBFI's money laundering and terrorist financing risk assessment or as recommended by the supervisory agency and/or the financial intelligence unit.

Responsibilities

Senior managers are responsible for the effective implementation of a risk-based approach to the management of money laundering and terrorist financing risk. The management of risk needs to be reviewed and updated from time to time to reflect changes in the NBFI's strategy or other factors such as changes to the law. Policies and procedures should take into account risk factors relating to the customer, product and service, delivery channel, and geographic location of the customer. Where higher risks are identified, based on the NBFI's risk assessment, the staff must take extra measures and senior management should ensure that the staff fully understand and implement the requirements of the policies and procedures.

Responsibilities and Roles of the Compliance Officer

The compliance officer is responsible for the following actions:

- Receiving inputs from staff and making suspicious transaction reports to the financial intelligence unit.
- Developing and maintaining the anti-money laundering and counterterrorist financing policy and internal procedures of the nonbank financial institution (NBFI) in line with legal requirements.
- Assisting the management in developing and maintaining an effective anti-money laundering and counterterrorist financing compliance culture.
- Ensuring adequate documentation of the NBFI's risk management policies regarding prevention of money laundering and terrorist financing, risk assessments, and their application.
- Determining and updating, in consultation with the senior management, a risk-based approach regarding money laundering and terrorist financing and the risk assessment of the NBFI's customers, products, services, delivery channels, and geographic reach.
- Ensuring that all internal suspicious activity reports received are investigated without delay.
- Submitting suspicious transaction reports to the financial intelligence unit.
- Providing initial and updated training for all relevant staff, including all staff who handle cash transactions, and customer payments and transactions.
- Providing awareness training to the staff and the senior management.
- Ensuring that the staff are aware of and complying with their obligations under the law and the NBFI's policies and procedures and that the basis for the risk-based approach to managing money laundering and terrorist financing risks is understood and applied.
- Presenting reports to the board, chief executive officer, and the senior management; making recommendations, if any, for action to remedy any deficiencies in the policies, procedures, systems, or controls and following up on those recommendations.[1]

---

[1] If these reporting requirements are relevant given the size of the NBFI.

- Representing the NBFI at all external agencies, for example, supervisory, regulatory, or law enforcement agencies.
- Conducting intraday review of all alerts regarding all incoming and outgoing payments and taking the necessary decisions on reported matches and false positives in relation to money laundering or terrorist financing.
- Ensuring that he or she is aware of any relevant sanctions and prohibition or advisory notices issued by the supervisory agency, the financial intelligence unit, or other agencies such as the United Nations Security Council.
- Responding promptly to any reasonable request for information from the supervisory, regulatory, and/or law enforcement agencies.
- Ensuring that the required screening of all new accounts, relationship updates, and ongoing updates of enhanced due diligence and risk assessment reports are carried out in accordance with the requirements of the NBFI's policy statement.
- Ensuring that an automated list of all high-risk customers is produced.[2]
- Ensuring that all required updates of the risk assessment reports and enhanced monitoring processes are adhered to.

2   If appropriate given the size of the NBFI.

Responsibilities and Roles of the Management

The management is responsible for the following actions:

- Assisting in establishing and maintaining an effective compliance culture within the nonbank financial institution (NBFI) to combat money laundering, terrorist financing, and other forms of financial crime(s).
- Ensuring that procedures regarding anti-money laundering and counterterrorist financing are part of operational procedures.
- Ensuring that all day-to-day procedures contained in this handbook are working successfully and are being correctly applied.
- Advising the compliance officer of any problems in procedures that have arisen and where changes to the procedures may be necessary to resolve those problems.
- Monitoring the effectiveness of the policies, procedures, systems, and controls within their relevant business areas and assisting in the preparation of relevant reports to the board.
- Assisting with the risk assessment of the NBFI's customers, counterparties, products, or services and ensuring that the risk assessment is kept up to date in the light of changing circumstances.
- Ensuring that the compliance officer is provided with any relevant customer, counterparty, or correspondent NBFI information available to them or their business units.
- Ensuring that the compliance officer is promptly advised where there are reasonable grounds to know or suspect that activity(ies), transactions, or instructions are linked to money laundering or terrorist financing.
- Ensuring that the staff for whom they are responsible understand the NBFI's risk-based approach toward preventing money laundering and terrorist financing, and that they apply it appropriately in their day-to-day operations.
- Ensuring that all the relevant staff receive training specifically tailored to their day-to-day activities in relation to money laundering and the financing of terrorism.

Responsibilities and Roles of the Staff

The staff is responsible for the following actions:

- Ensuring that no action is undertaken on behalf of a customer without a clear understanding of the purpose and background of the transaction(s) or activity(ies).
- Reporting promptly to the compliance officer when they have knowledge or suspicion of money laundering or the financing of terrorism or where there are reasonable grounds to know of or suspect money laundering or terrorist financing.
- Not tipping off any customer or any person that a suspicious transaction report has been made or that their account and/or transactions are under investigation either internally by the compliance officer or externally by the financial intelligence unit.
- Assisting fully with any investigation.
- Completing a record of when they have received anti-money laundering training and the nature of that training.

Example of a Risk Assessment Form

Anti-Money Laundering and Combating the Financing of Terrorism—Risk-Based Approach Matrix

Customer types

Note: All accounts are subject to a variety of risk "scores" on various factors, e.g., client, product, location, and delivery channels to form an overall scoring.

	High	Medium	Low
Personal Customers (resident and nonresident)			
Individual customers (consider other factors, e.g., geographic risk, employment status)			
Students and minors			
Politically exposed persons (PEPs) (Note: *Rated "High" subject to frequent checks*)			
Non-Personal Customers (resident and nonresident)			
Publicly quoted companies			
Private companies			
Charities, church, nonprofit organizations, etc.			
Other regulated financial firms subject to money laundering and terrorist financing regulations			
Other firms subject to money laundering and terrorist financing regulations			
Correspondent banks			
Partnerships and unincorporated businesses			
Clubs and societies			

Public sector bodies, governments (including central government), and state-owned companies			
Sole traders			
Offshore trusts and foundations			
Embassies			
International organizations			
Others			
One-off transactions for non-account holders			
New accounts (opened within 1 year) (depends on other factors)			
Accounts operated under power of attorney			
When conducting an assessment where beneficial owners, directors, or third parties are present, then consider information on that person			

Product, Delivery Channels, and Geographic Risk Anti-Money Laundering

	High	Medium	Low
Product			
Current accounts, cash			
Overdrafts			
Fixed deposits			
Foreign exchange			
Treasury			
Trade finance (depends upon location)			
Commercial lending			

Delivery Channels			
Products applied for or services provided face to face			
Products applied for remotely			
Location			
List geographic regions where customers are based and transfer funds to or from.			

Risk Assessment Calculator

Criteria	Overall Score
2 high in any one category	High
1 high in any one category	Medium
2 medium in any one category	Medium
1 medium in any one category	Medium/Low

The calculation formula is to be used as a general guideline only; staff should take a view in each case and assign an appropriate risk rating which could be higher or lower than the calculated formula. Please state reasons.

Example of an Account Opening Checklist—Individuals

(When completed, please attach to account opening form)

Full name:
Account number:
1. Specimen signature card:
2. Proof of permanent residential address, not older than 3 months: e.g., utility bill—electricity, gas, fixed line telephone (not mobile); *please state which*
3. Introduction letter if the account is requested on a non–face-to-face basis from one of: - the applicant's bankers   - other person/entity accepted by the nonbank financial institution
4. Face-to-face applicants: take sight of the applicant's <u>original valid passport</u> and   - take photocopy of the original passport,   - certify the photocopy of the original passport as a true copy, and   - certify the photocopy of the applicant's photograph as a true likeness
5. Bank statements—3 months' statements, within the past 5 months
6. Unique static identification number: (National Insurance Number or Tax Identification Number)
7. Purpose of account:
8. Nationality.   Dual nationality?   Yes/No   If yes, passport <u>copies</u> taken   Note for the staff opening the account: Are there any other indications of the customer having business activities in other countries?
9. Source of funds/income (wealth): investments, shares held, value of property
10. Expected receipts and movements over the account:
11. Is the customer a politically exposed person?   Yes/No/Unsure (delete as appropriate)   Check of databases has been performed:

12. If the applicant wishes to issue a power of attorney on the applicant's account, obtain the following:
- reason for power of attorney
- proof of the permanent residential address of the power of attorney
- proof of identity of power of attorney by sight of original passport and certification of copy(ies)

Completed by (staff member): _ _ _ _ _ _ _ _   Date:_ _ / _ _ / _ _ _ _

(When completed, please attach to account opening form)

Full name:
Account number:
1. Certificate of incorporation
2. Board resolution/mandate to open an account
3. Memorandum of articles and association
4. Registration of address
5. Company structure, e.g., organization chart
6. Ultimate ownership or beneficial ownership
7. Names of all directors, controllers, and signatories
8. Latest audited accounts
9. Call report and business case report containing the purpose of opening the account, expected movements over the account, and all recommendations for the account
10. Copy and declaration of money laundering procedures
11. For private companies: names of beneficial owners holding over 25% of the shares
12. For private companies: source of wealth statement for politically exposed persons and/or beneficial owners
13. Certified list of signatories and identification of controllers/directors, i.e., passports, proof of address

Completed by (staff member): _ _ _ _ _ _ _ _   Date:_ _ / _ _ / _ _ _ _

Examples of Suspicious Transactions

Common indicators

The following are examples of common indicators that may point to a suspicious transaction, whether completed or attempted. This list of examples is provided for guidance only and is neither mandatory nor exhaustive.[1]

General areas of suspicion

- Customer admits to or makes statements about involvement in criminal activities.
- You are aware that a customer is the subject of a criminal investigation.
- Customer does not want correspondence sent to residential address.
- Customer appears to have accounts with several financial institutions in one area for no apparent reason.
- Customer conducts transactions at different physical locations in an apparent attempt to avoid detection.
- Customer repeatedly uses an address but frequently changes the names involved.

[1] The information provided in this appendix has been reproduced with the kind permission of the Financial Transactions and Reports Analysis Centre of Canada (FINTRAC). The list is an excerpt from FINTRAC's *Guideline 2 – Suspicious Transactions* which was published in July 2016. The full version of the guideline can be found online (at http://www.fintrac-canafe.gc.ca/publications/ guide/Guide2/2-eng.asp). The list reproduced in this appendix is not exhaustive and may be out of date. The reproduction of the material in this appendix has not been produced in affiliation with, or with the endorsement of, FINTRAC.

- Customer is accompanied and watched.
- Significant and/or frequent transactions in contrast to known or expected business activity(ies).
- Significant and/or frequent transactions in contrast to known employment status.
- Ambiguous or inconsistent explanations as to the source and/or purpose of funds.
- Where relevant, money presented in unusual condition, for example, damp, odorous, or coated with substance.
- Where relevant, nervous or uncooperative behavior exhibited by employees and/or customers.
- Customer shows uncommon curiosity about internal systems, controls, and policies.
- Customer has only vague knowledge of the amount of a deposit.
- Customer presents confusing details about the transaction or knows few details about its purpose.
- Customer appears to informally record large-volume transactions, using unconventional bookkeeping methods or "off-the-record" books.
- Customer over-justifies or -explains the transaction.
- Customer is secretive and reluctant to meet in person.
- Customer is nervous, not in keeping with the transaction.
- Customer is involved in transactions that are suspicious but seems blind to being involved in money-laundering activities.
- Customer's home or business telephone number has been disconnected, or there is no such number when an attempt is made to contact the customer shortly after opening the account.
- Normal attempts to verify the background of a new or prospective customer are difficult.
- Customer appears to be acting on behalf of a third party but does not inform the credit institution staff.
- Customer is involved in activity(ies) out of keeping for that individual or business.
- Customer insists that a transaction be done quickly.
- Inconsistencies appear in the customer's presentation of the transaction.
- Transaction does not appear to make sense or is out of keeping with usual or expected activity for the customer.
- Customer appears to have recently established a series of new relationships with different financial entities.
- Customer attempts to develop close rapport with the staff.

- Customer uses aliases and a variety of similar but different addresses.
- Customer spells his or her name differently from one transaction to another.
- Customer uses a post office box or general delivery address, or other type of mail drop address, instead of a street address when this is not the norm for the area concerned.
- Customer provides false information or information that the staff of the bank or the financial institution believe is unreliable.
- Customer offers money, gratuities, or unusual favors to the credit institution staff for the provision of services that may appear unusual or suspicious.
- Customer pays for services or products via financial instruments, such as money orders or traveler's checks, without relevant entries on the instrument or with unusual symbols, stamps, or notes.
- The bank or the financial institution is aware that a customer is the subject of a money laundering or terrorist financing investigation.
- The bank or the financial institution is aware, or becomes aware, from a reliable source (that can include media or other open sources) that a customer is suspected of being involved in illegal activity(ies).
- A new or prospective customer is known as having a questionable legal reputation or criminal background.
- Transaction involves a suspected shell entity (i.e., a corporation that has no assets, operations, or other reasons to exist).

Knowledge of reporting or record-keeping requirements

- Customer attempts to convince employee not to complete any documentation required for the transaction.
- Customer makes inquiries that would indicate a desire to avoid reporting.
- Customer has unusual knowledge of the law in relation to suspicious transaction reporting.
- Customer seems very conversant with money laundering or terrorist activity financing issues.
- Customer is quick to volunteer that funds are "clean" or are "not being laundered."

- Customer appears to be structuring amounts to avoid record keeping, customer identification, or reporting thresholds.
- Customer appears to be collaborating with others to avoid record keeping, customer identification, or reporting thresholds.
- Customer performs two or more cash transactions of less than the thresholds specified seemingly to avoid the reporting requirement.

Identity documents

- Customer provides doubtful or vague information.
- Customer produces seemingly false identification or identification that appears to be counterfeited, altered, or inaccurate.
- Customer refuses to produce personal identification documents.
- Customer only presents copies rather than originals.
- Customer uses foreign, unverifiable identity documents.
- Customer wants to establish identity using something other than his or her personal identification documents.
- Customer's supporting documentation lacks important details, such as a telephone number.
- Customer inordinately delays presenting corporate documents.
- All identification presented pertains to foreign countries or cannot be checked for some reason.
- All identification documents presented appear new or have recent issue dates.
- Customer presents different identification documents at different times.
- Customer alters the transaction after being asked for identity documents.
- Customer presents different identification documents each time a transaction is conducted.

Cash transactions

- Customer starts conducting frequent cash transactions in large amounts when this has not been a normal activity for the customer in the past.
- Customer frequently exchanges small bills for large ones.
- Customer uses notes in denominations that are unusual for the customer, when the normal practice in that business is different.
- Customer presents notes that are packed or wrapped in a way that is uncommon for the customer.
- Customer deposits musty or extremely dirty bills.
- Customer consistently makes cash transactions that are just under the reporting threshold amount in an apparent attempt to avoid the reporting threshold.
- Customer consistently makes cash transactions that are significantly below the reporting threshold amount in an apparent attempt to avoid triggering the identification and reporting requirements.
- Customer presents uncounted funds for a transaction. Upon counting, the customer reduces the transaction to an amount just below that which could trigger reporting requirements.
- Customer conducts a transaction for an amount that is unusual compared with amounts of past transactions.
- Customer frequently purchases traveler's checks, foreign currency drafts, or other negotiable instruments with cash when this appears to be outside of normal activity for the customer.
- Customer asks a clerk at the credit institution to hold or transmit large sums of money or other assets when this type of activity is unusual for the customer.
- Shared address for individuals involved in cash transactions, particularly when the address is also for a business location, or does not seem to correspond to the stated occupation (i.e., student, unemployed, self-employed, etc.).
- Stated occupation of the customer is not in keeping with the level or type of activity(ies) (e.g., a student or an unemployed individual makes daily maximum cash withdrawals at multiple locations over a wide geographic area).
- Cash is transported by a cash courier.
- Large transactions using a variety of denominations.

Economic purpose

- Transaction seems to be inconsistent with the customer's apparent financial standing or the usual pattern of activities.
- Transaction appears to be out of the normal course for industry practice or does not appear to be economically viable for the customer.
- Transaction is unnecessarily complex for its stated purpose.
- Activity is inconsistent with what would be expected from declared business.
- A business customer refuses to provide information to qualify for a business discount.
- No business explanation for size of transactions or cash volumes.
- Transactions or financial connections between businesses that are not usually connected (e.g., a food importer dealing with an automobile parts exporter).
- Transaction involves nonprofit or charitable organization(s) for which there appears to be no logical economic purpose or where there appears to be no link between the stated activity(ies) of the organization and the other parties in the transaction.

Transactions involving accounts

- Opening accounts when the customer's address is outside the local service area.
- Opening accounts in other people's names.
- Opening accounts with names very close to other established business entities.
- Attempting to open or operate accounts under a false name.

- Account with a large number of small cash deposits and a small number of large cash withdrawals.
- Funds are being deposited into several accounts, consolidated into one, and transferred outside the country.
- Customer frequently uses many deposit locations outside of the home branch location.

- Multiple transactions are carried out on the same day at the same branch but with an apparent attempt to use different tellers.
- Activity far exceeds activity projected at the time of opening of the account.
- Establishment of multiple accounts, some of which appear to remain dormant for extended periods.
- Account that was reactivated from inactive or dormant status suddenly sees significant activity.
- Reactivated dormant account containing a minimal amount suddenly receives a deposit or series of deposits followed by frequent cash withdrawals until the transferred sum has been removed.
- Unexplained transfers between the customer's products and accounts.
- Large transfers from one account to other accounts that appear to be pooling money from different sources.
- Multiple deposits are made to a customer's account by third parties.
- Deposits or withdrawals of multiple monetary instruments, particularly if the instruments are sequentially numbered.
- Frequent deposits of bearer instruments (e.g., checks, money orders, or bearer bonds) in amounts just below the threshold amount.
- Unusually large cash deposits by a customer with personal or business links to an area associated with drug trafficking.
- Regular return of checks for insufficient funds.
- Correspondent accounts being used as "pass-through" points from foreign jurisdictions with subsequent outgoing funds to another foreign jurisdiction.
- Multiple personal and business accounts are used to collect and then funnel funds to a small number of foreign beneficiaries, particularly when they are in locations of concern, such as countries known or suspected to facilitate money-laundering activities.

Transactions involving areas outside the country

- Customer and other parties to the transaction have no apparent ties to the country.
- Transaction crosses many international lines.
- Use of a credit card issued by a foreign bank that does not operate domestically by a customer who does not live and work in the country of issue.
- Cash volumes and international remittances in excess of average income for migrant worker customers.

- Transactions involving high-volume international transfers to third-party accounts in countries that are not usual remittance corridors.
- Transaction involves a country known for highly secretive banking and corporate law(s).
- Foreign currency exchanges that are associated with subsequent wire transfers to locations of concern, such as countries known or suspected to facilitate money-laundering activities.
- Deposits followed within a short time by wire transfer of funds to or through locations of concern, such as countries known or suspected to facilitate money-laundering activities.
- Transaction involves a country where illicit drug production or exporting may be prevalent, or where there is no effective anti-money laundering system.
- Transaction involves a country known or suspected to facilitate money-laundering activities.

Transactions related to offshore business activity

Any bank or financial institution that conducts transactions internationally should consider the following indicators:

- Accumulation of large balances, inconsistent with the known turnover of the customer's business, and subsequent transfers to overseas account(s).
- Frequent requests for traveler's checks, foreign currency drafts, or other negotiable instruments.
- Loans secured by obligations from offshore banks.
- Loans to or from offshore companies.

- Offers of multimillion-dollar deposits from a confidential source to be sent from an offshore bank or somehow guaranteed by an offshore bank.
- Transactions involving an offshore "shell" bank whose name may be very similar to the name of a major legitimate institution.
- Unexplained electronic funds transfers by customer on an in-and-out basis.
- Use of letter of credit and other methods of trade financing to move money between countries when such trade is inconsistent with the customer's business.
- Use of a credit card issued by an offshore bank.

Personal transactions

- Customer appears to have accounts with several financial institutions in one geographic area.
- Customer has no employment history but makes frequent, large transactions or maintains a large account balance.
- The flow of income through the account does not match what was expected based on the stated occupation of the account holder or the intended use of the account.
- Customer makes one or more cash deposits to the general account of a foreign correspondent bank (i.e., pass-through account).
- Customer makes frequent or large payments through online payment services.
- Customer runs large positive credit card balances.
- Customer uses cash advances from a credit card account to purchase money orders or drafts or to wire funds to foreign destinations.
- Customer takes cash advance to deposit into savings or checking account.
- Large cash payments for outstanding credit card balances.
- Customer makes credit card overpayment and then requests a cash advance.
- Customer visits the safety deposit box area immediately before making cash deposits.
- Customer wishes to have credit and debit cards sent to international or to domestic destinations other than his or her address.
- Customer has numerous accounts and deposits cash into each of them with the total credits being a large amount.
- Customer deposits large endorsed checks in the name of a third party.

- Customer frequently makes deposits to the account of another individual who is not an employee or family member.
- Customer frequently exchanges currencies.
- Customer frequently makes automatic banking machine deposits just below the reporting threshold.
- Customer's access of the safety deposit facilities increases substantially or is unusual in light of their past usage.
- Many unrelated individuals make payments to one account without any rational explanation.
- Third parties make cash payments or deposit checks to a customer's credit card.
- Customer gives power of attorney to a nonrelative to conduct large transactions.
- Customer has frequent deposits identified as proceeds of asset sales, but the assets cannot be substantiated.
- Customer acquires significant assets and liquidates them quickly with no explanation.
- Customer acquires significant assets and encumbers them with security interests that do not make economic sense.
- Customer requests movement of funds that are uneconomical.
- High volume of wire transfers are made or received through the account.

Corporate and business transactions

Some businesses may be susceptible to the mixing of illicit funds with legitimate income. This is a very common method of money laundering. These businesses include those that conduct a significant part of their business in cash, such as restaurants, bars, parking lots, convenience stores, and vending machine companies. On opening accounts with the various businesses in its area, a financial institution would likely be aware of those that are mainly cash based.

- Unusual or unexplained increases in cash deposits made by those entities may be indicative of suspicious activity(ies).

- Accounts are used to receive or disburse large sums but show virtually no normal business-related activities such as the payment of payrolls, invoices, etc.
- Accounts have a large volume of deposits in bank drafts, cashier's checks, money orders, or electronic funds transfers, which is inconsistent with the customer's business.
- Accounts have deposits in combinations of monetary instruments that are atypical of legitimate business activity(ies) (e.g., deposits that include a mix of business, payroll, and social security checks).
- Accounts have deposits in combinations of cash and monetary instruments not normally associated with business activity(ies).
- Business does not want to provide complete information regarding its activities.
- Financial statements of the business differ noticeably from those of similar businesses.
- Representatives of the business avoid contact with the branch as much as possible, even when it would be more convenient for them.
- Deposits to or withdrawals from a corporate account are primarily in cash rather than in the form of debit and credit normally associated with commercial operations.
- Customer maintains a number of trustee or customer accounts that are not consistent with that type of business or not in keeping with normal industry practices.
- Customer operates a retail business providing check-cashing services but does not make large withdrawals of cash against checks deposited.
- Customer pays in cash or deposits cash to cover bank drafts, money transfers, or other negotiable and marketable money instruments.
- Customer purchases cashier's checks and money orders with large amounts of cash.
- Customer deposits large amounts of currency wrapped in currency straps.
- Customer makes a large volume of seemingly unrelated deposits to several accounts and frequently transfers a major portion of the balances to a single account at the same bank or elsewhere.
- Customer makes a large volume of cash deposits from a business that is not normally cash-intensive.
- Customer makes large cash withdrawals from a business account not normally associated with cash transactions.

- Customer consistently makes immediate large withdrawals from an account that has just received a large and unexpected credit from abroad.
- Customer makes a single and substantial cash deposit composed of many large bills.
- Small, single location business makes deposits on the same day at different branches across a broad geographic area that does not appear practical for the business.
- There is a substantial increase in deposits of cash or negotiable instruments by a company offering professional advisory services, especially if the deposits are promptly transferred.
- There is a sudden change in cash transactions or patterns.
- Customer wishes to have credit and debit cards sent to international or domestic destinations other than his or her place of business.
- There is a marked increase in transaction volume in an account with significant changes in an account balance that is inconsistent with or not in keeping with normal business practices of the customer's account.
- Asset acquisition is accompanied by security arrangements that are not consistent with normal practice.
- Unexplained transactions are repeated between personal and commercial accounts.
- Activity is inconsistent with stated business.
- Account has close connections with other business accounts without any apparent reason for the connection.
- Activity suggests that transactions may offend securities regulations or the business prospectus is not in tune with the requirements.
- A large number of incoming and outgoing wire transfers take place for which there appears to be no logical business or other economic purpose, particularly when this is through or from locations of concern, such as countries known or suspected to facilitate money-laundering activities.

Transactions for nonprofit organizations (including registered charities)

- Inconsistencies between apparent modest sources of funds of the organization (e.g., communities with modest standard of living) and large amounts of funds raised.
- Inconsistencies between the pattern or size of financial transactions and the stated purpose and activity of the organization.

- Sudden increase in the frequency and amounts of financial transactions for the organization, or the inverse, that is, the organization seems to hold funds in its account for a very long period.
- Large and unexplained cash transactions by the organization.
- Absence of contributions from donors located in the country.
- Organization's directors are outside the country, particularly if large outgoing transactions are made to the country of origin of the directors and especially if that country is a high-risk jurisdiction.

- Large number of nonprofit organizations with unexplained links.
- Nonprofit organization appears to have little or no staff, no suitable offices, or no telephone number, which is incompatible with their stated purpose and financial flows.
- Nonprofit organization has operations in, or conducts transactions to or from, high-risk jurisdictions.

Wire and funds transfer activities

- Customer is reluctant to give an explanation for the remittance.
- Customer orders wire transfers in small amounts in an apparent effort to avoid triggering identification or reporting requirements.
- Customer receives large sums of money from an overseas location and the transfers include regulations for payment in cash.
- Customer makes frequent or large funds transfers for individuals or entities who have no account relationship with the institution.
- Customer receives frequent funds transfers from individuals or entities who have no account relationship with the institution.
- Customer receives funds transfers and immediately purchases monetary instruments prepared for payment to a third party, which is inconsistent with or is outside the normal course of business of the customer.
- Customer requests payment in cash immediately upon receipt of a large funds transfer.
- Customer instructs the bank or the financial institution to transfer funds abroad and to expect an equal incoming transfer.

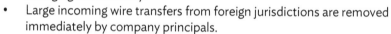

- Immediately after transferred funds have cleared, the customer moves the funds to another account or to another individual or entity.
- Customer shows unusual interest in funds transfer systems and questions the limit of what amount can be transferred.
- Customer transfers funds to another country without changing the currency.
- Large incoming wire transfers from foreign jurisdictions are removed immediately by company principals.
- Customer sends frequent wire transfers to foreign countries but does not seem to have connection to such countries.
- Wire transfers are received from entities having no apparent business connection with the customer.
- Size of funds transfers is inconsistent with normal business transactions for that customer.
- Rising volume of remittances exceeds what was expected from the customer when the relationship was established.
- Several customers request transfers either on the same day or over a period of 2–3 days to the same recipient.
- Different customers request transfers that are all paid for by the same customer.
- Several customers requesting transfers share common identifiers, such as family name, address, or telephone number.
- Several different customers send transfers that are similar in amounts, sender names, test questions, free message text, and destination country.
- Customer sends or receives multiple transfers to or from the same individual.
- Stated occupation of the customer or the customer's financial standing is not in keeping with the level or type of activity(ies) (e.g., a student or an unemployed individual who receives or sends large numbers of wire transfers).
- Migrant remittances made outside the usual remittance corridors.
- Personal funds sent at a time not associated with salary payments.
- Country of destination for a wire transfer is not consistent with the nationality of the individual customer.

- Customer requests transfers to a large number of recipients outside the country who do not appear to be family members.
- Customer does not appear to know the recipient to whom he or she is sending the transfer.
- Customer does not appear to know the sender of the transfer from whom the transfer was received.
- Beneficiaries of wire transfers involve a large group of nationals of countries associated with terrorist activity.
- Customer makes funds transfers to other businesses abroad that are not in line with the customer's business.
- Customer conducts transactions involving countries known as narcotic source countries or as transshipment points for narcotics, or that are known for highly secretive banking and corporate law practices.

Suspicious indicators related to lending

- Customer suddenly repays a problem loan unexpectedly.
- Customer makes a large, unexpected loan payment with unknown source of funds, or a source of funds that does not match the credit institution's knowledge about the customer.
- Customer repays a long-term loan, such as a mortgage, within a relatively short time period.
- Source of down payment is inconsistent with borrower's background and income.
- Down payment appears to be from an unrelated third party.
- Down payment uses a series of money orders or bank drafts from different financial institutions.
- Customer shows income from "foreign sources" on loan application without providing further details.
- Customer's employment documentation lacks important details that would make it difficult for the credit institution to contact or locate the employer.
- Customer's documentation to ascertain identification, support income, or verify employment is provided by an intermediary who has no apparent reason to be involved.

- Customer has loans with offshore institutions or companies that are outside the ordinary course of business of the customer.
- Customer offers the credit institution large dollar deposits or some other form of incentive in return for favorable treatment of loan request.
- Customer asks to borrow against assets held by another financial institution or a third party, when the origin of the assets is not known.
- Loan transaction does not make economic sense (e.g., the customer has significant assets, and there does not appear to be a sound business reason for the transaction).
- Customer seems unconcerned with terms of credit or costs associated with completion of a loan transaction.
- Customer applies for loans on the strength of a financial statement reflecting major investments in or income from businesses incorporated in countries known for highly secretive banking and corporate law(s) and the application is outside the ordinary course of business of the customer.
- Down payment or other loan payments are made by a party who is not a relative of the customer.
- Reluctance to use favorable facilities, for example, avoiding high interest rate facilities for large balances.
- Substantial increases in deposits of cash or negotiable instruments by a professional firm or company, using customer accounts, in-house company, or trust accounts, especially if the deposits are promptly transferred between other customer companies and trust accounts.
- Frequent and/or unscheduled cash deposits to loan accounts.
- Frequent deposits of winning gambling checks followed by immediate withdrawal or transfer of funds.
- Children's accounts being used for the benefit of parents and/or guardians.

Life insurance companies, brokers, and agents

- Client wants to use cash for a large transaction.
- Client proposes to purchase an insurance product using a check drawn on an account other than his or her personal account.
- Client requests an insurance product that has no discernible purpose and is reluctant to divulge the reason for the investment.
- Client who has other small policies or transactions based on a regular payment structure makes a sudden request to purchase a substantial policy with a lump-sum payment.

- Client conducts a transaction that results in a conspicuous increase in investment contributions.
- Scale of investment in insurance products is inconsistent with the client's economic profile.
- Unanticipated and inconsistent modification of client's contractual conditions, including significant or regular premium top-ups.
- Unforeseen deposit of funds or abrupt withdrawal of funds.
- Involvement of one or more third parties in paying the premiums or in any other matters involving the policy.
- Overpayment of a policy premium with a subsequent request to refund the surplus to a third party.
- Funds used to pay policy premiums or deposits originate from different sources.
- Use of life insurance product in a way that resembles the use of a bank account, such as making additional premium payments and frequent partial redemptions.
- Client cancels investment or insurance soon after purchase.
- Early redemption takes place in the absence of a reasonable explanation or in a significantly uneconomic manner.
- Client shows more interest in the cancellation or surrender of an insurance contract than in the long-term results of investments or the costs associated with termination of the contract.
- Client makes payments with small denomination notes, uncommonly wrapped, with postal money orders or with similar means of payment.
- Duration of the life insurance contract is less than 3 years.
- First (or single) premium is paid from a bank account outside the country.
- Client accepts very unfavorable conditions unrelated to his or her health or age.
- Transaction involves use and payment of a performance bond resulting in a cross-border payment.
- Repeated and unexplained changes in beneficiary.
- Relationship between the policy holder and the beneficiary is not clearly established.

Securities firms

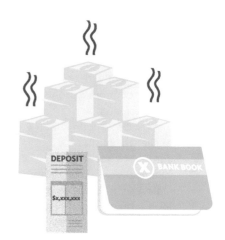

- Accounts that have been inactive suddenly receive large deposits that are inconsistent with the normal investment practice of the client or their financial ability.
- Any dealing with a third party when the identity of the beneficiary or counterparty is undisclosed.
- Client attempts to purchase investments with cash.
- Client wishes to purchase a number of investments with money orders, traveler's checks, cashier's checks, bank drafts, or other bank instruments, where the transaction is inconsistent with the normal investment practice of the client or their financial ability.
- Client uses securities or futures brokerage firm as a place to hold funds that are not being used in trading of securities or futures for an extended period of time, and such activity is inconsistent with the normal investment practice of the client or their financial ability.
- Client wishes monies received through the sale of shares to be deposited into a bank account rather than a trading or brokerage account, which is inconsistent with the normal practice of the client.
- Client frequently makes large investments in stocks, bonds, investment trusts, or other securities in cash or by check within a short time period, inconsistent with the normal practice of the client.
- Client makes large or unusual settlements of securities in cash.
- The entry of matching buying and selling of particular securities or futures contracts (called match trading), creating the illusion of trading.
- Transfers of funds or securities between accounts not known to be related to the client.
- Several clients open accounts within a short period of time to trade the same stock.
- Unrelated clients redirect funds toward the same account.

- Trades conducted by entities that you know have been named or sanctioned by regulators in the past for irregular or inappropriate trading activity(ies).
- Client is willing to deposit or invest at rates that are not advantageous or competitive.
- Client attempts to purchase investments with instruments in the name of a third party.
- Third-party purchases of shares in other names (i.e., nominee accounts).
- Transactions in which clients make settlements with checks drawn by third parties or remittances from third parties.
- Proposed transactions are to be funded by international wire payments, particularly if from countries where there is no effective anti-money laundering system.

L isted below are a number of websites that may assist entities in the development of anti-money laundering and combating the financing of terrorism (AML/CFT) risk management systems. In addition to these websites, a number of supervisory agencies have produced handbooks designed to assist entities understand and implement their obligations in relation to combating money laundering and the financing of terrorism and proliferation. These handbooks and other guidance materials can be found on the internet. As with this handbook, the handbooks online provide useful guidance to assist entities in the development of effective AML/CFT risk management systems. However, neither this handbook nor handbooks developed by supervisory agencies are intended to detail an exhaustive list of recommended AML/CFT controls. Each firm must consider its own individual circumstances given the range of products and services it offers and the types of customers that seek to transact with the entity.

There are also a number of websites that provide general information on money laundering and the financing of terrorism. These websites provide definitions of common terms, give information on the consequences of failing to combat money laundering and the financing of terrorism, and provide information on typologies related to money laundering and the financing of terrorism which may assist entities to better understand potential money laundering and terrorist financing risks.

The Financial Action Task Force (FATF) is the international standard setter that develops and promotes policies to protect the global financial system against money laundering, terrorist financing, and the financing of proliferation of weapons of mass destruction. The FATF has issued a number of guidance papers which could be used to assist entities understand money laundering and terrorist financing risks. These papers and other materials can be found online (at http://www.fatgt-gafi.org). Additional materials can also be found on the website of the Asia/Pacific Group on Money Laundering (at http://www.apgml.org).

The Financial Transactions and Reports Analysis Centre of Canada (FINTRAC), Canada's financial intelligence unit, provides guidance and information in relation to the obligations placed on entities in relation to the fight against money laundering and terrorist financing. FINTRAC's website (http://www.fintrac-canafe.gc.ca/) provides information designed to assist a range of entities comply with their obligations and includes a list of examples of indicators of suspicion and examples of industry-specific suspicious transactions which can be of use to entities when developing their own indicators of suspicion and for the training of staff.

The Australian Transaction Reports and Analysis Centre is Australia's financial intelligence unit. Its website (http://www.austrac.gov.au) provides information for entities to assist them to meet their obligations in relation to money laundering and terrorist financing. The website includes examples of suspicious transactions and guidance on the development of internal risk management policies and procedures that entities should implement to ensure that they are effectively managing their money laundering and terrorist financing risks.

The Joint Money Laundering Steering Group is made up of leading trade associations in the financial services industry in the United Kingdom. The group provides guidance for the finance sector in the United Kingdom on how to meet their obligations in relation to combating money laundering and the financing of terrorism. Its website (http://www.jmlsg.org.uk) provides guidance that could assist entities in developing AML/CFT risk management policies and procedures.

The Basel Committee on Banking Supervision, which is the primary standard setter for the prudential regulation of banks, has issued a set of guidelines which can be found online (http://www.bis.org/bcbs/publ/d353.htm) to describe how banks should include risks related to money laundering and financing of terrorism within their overall risk management framework. These guidelines, while focusing on banks, provide useful guidance to entities when developing a framework to manage their money laundering and financing of terrorism risks.

The International Association of Insurance Supervisors is the international standard-setting body responsible for developing and assisting in the implementation of principles, standards, and other supporting material for the supervision of the insurance sector. The association has issued guidance which explains the vulnerability of the insurance sector with respect to money laundering and terrorist financing and provides case studies on money laundering. It presents measures and procedures to control these risks, including customer due diligence. The paper can be found online (http://www .iaisweb.org/page/supervisory-material/guidance-papers).

The International Organization of Securities Commissions (IOSCO) in its principles paper and related documents has outlined requirements in relation to combating money laundering and the financing of terrorism. The paper can be found online (http://www.iosco.org/library/pubdocs/pdf/IOSCOPD359 .pdf) and includes references and links to other IOSCO publications that deal with money laundering and the financing of terrorism.

References

Australian Transaction Reports and Analysis Centre. http://www.austrac.gov.au

———. *Compliance Guide.* http://www.austrac.gov.au/businesses/obligations
-and-compliance/austrac-compliance-guide

Basel Committee on Banking Supervision. http://www.bis.org

———. 2014. *Sound Management of the Risks Related to Money Laundering and
Financing of Terrorism.* http://www.bis.org/bcbs/publ/d353.pdf

———. 2016. *General Guide to Account Opening.* http://www.bis.org/bcbs/
publ/d353.htm

Financial Action Task Force. 2012. *International Standards on Combating
Money Laundering and the Financing of Terrorism and Proliferation.* http://
www.fatf-gafi.org/publications/fatfrecommendations/documents/fatf
-recommendations.html

Financial Transactions and Reports Analysis Centre of Canada. http://www
.fintrac-canafe.gc.ca

———. 2016. *Guideline 2, Suspicious Transactions.* http://www.fintrac-canafe
.gc.ca/publications/guide/Guide2/2-eng.asp

———. 2016. Guideline 4, *Implementation of a Compliance Regime.* http://
www.fintrac-canafe.gc.ca/publications/guide/Guide4/4-eng.asp

International Association of Insurance Supervisors. http://www.iaisweb.org

———. 2004. *Guidance Paper on Anti-Money Laundering and Combatting
the Financing of Terrorism.* http://www.iaisweb.org/page/supervisory
-material/guidance-papers/file/34267/5-guidance-paper-on-anti
-money-laundering-and-combating-the-financing-of-terrorism
-october-2004-updated-title

International Organization of Securities Commissions. http://iosco.org

————. 1992. *Report on Money Laundering.* http://www.iosco.org/library/ pubdocs/pdf/IOSCOPD26.pdf

Joint Money Laundering Steering Group. http://www.jmlsg.org.uk

————. 2014. *Prevention of Money Laundering/Terrorist Financing (Part 1).* http://www.jmlsg.org.uk/download/9803

————. 2014. *Prevention of Money Laundering/Terrorist Financing (Part 2).* http://www.jmlsg.org.uk/download/9804

Printed in the USA
CPSIA information can be obtained
at www.ICGtesting.com
LVHW070855061023
760002LV00005B/228